The

Stark Munro

Letters

Edited and arranged by

Sir A. Conan Doyle

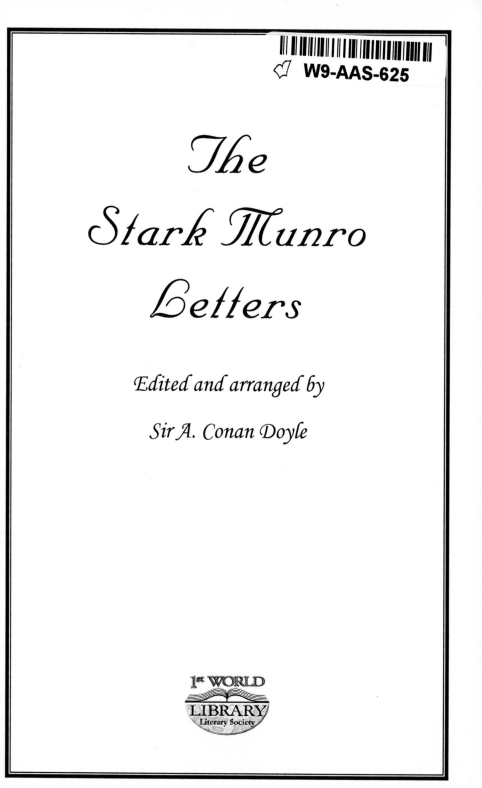

1st WORLD
LIBRARY
Literary Society

The Stark Munro Letters
Edited and arranged by
Sir Arthur Conan Doyle

© 1st World Library – Literary Society, 2004
PO Box 2211
Fairfield, IA 52556
www.1stworldlibrary.org
First Edition

LCCN: 2003195089

ISBN: 1-59540-415-5

Purchase *"The Stark Munro Letters"*
as a traditional bound book at:
www.1stWorldLibrary.org/purchase.asp?ISBN=1-59540-415-5

1st World Library Literary Society is a nonprofit
organization dedicated to promoting literacy by:

- Creating a free internet library accessible from any computer worldwide.
- Hosting writing competitions and offering book publishing scholarships.

Readers interested in supporting literacy
through sponsorship, donations or
membership please contact:
literacy@1stworldlibrary.org
Check us out at: www.1stworldlibrary.org

The Stark Munro Letters
contributed by the Charles Family
in support of
1st World Library - Literary Society

THE STARK MUNRO LETTERS

BEING A SERIES OF TWELVE LETTERS
WRITTEN BY J. STARK MUNRO, M.B.,
TO HIS FRIEND AND FORMER FELLOW
STUDENT, HERBERT SWANBOROUGH,
OF LOWELL, MASSACHUSETTS,
DURING THE YEARS 1881-1884

EDITED AND ARRANGED BY
A. CONAN DOYLE

The letters of my friend Mr. Stark Munro appear to me to form so connected a whole, and to give so plain an account of some of the troubles which a young man may be called upon to face right away at the outset of his career, that I have handed them over to the gentleman who is about to edit them. There are two of them, the fifth and the ninth, from which some excisions are necessary; but in the main I hope that they may be reproduced as they stand. I am sure that there is no privilege which my friend would value more highly than the thought that some other young man, harassed by the needs of this world and doubts of the next, should have gotten strength by reading how a brother had passed down the valley of shadow before him.

HERBERT SWANBOROUGH.

LOWELL, MASS.

I

HOME.
30th March, 1881.

I have missed you very much since `your return to America, my dear Bertie, for you are the one man upon this earth to whom I have ever been able to unreservedly open my whole mind. I don't know why it is; for, now that I come to think of it, I have never enjoyed very much of your confidence in return. But that may be my fault. Perhaps you don't find me sympathetic, even though I have every wish to be. I can only say that I find you intensely so, and perhaps I presume too much upon the fact. But no, every instinct in my nature tells me that I don't bore you by my confidences.

Can you remember Cullingworth at the University? You never were in the athletic set, and so it is possible that you don't. Anyway, I'll take it for granted that you don't, and explain it all from the beginning. I'm sure that you would know his photograph, however, for the reason that he was the ugliest and queerest-looking man of our year.

Physically he was a fine athlete - one of the fastest and most determined Rugby forwards that I have ever known, though he played so savage a game that he was never given his international cap. He was well-grown, five foot nine perhaps, with square shoulders, an arching chest, and a quick jerky way of walking. He had a round strong head, bristling with short wiry black hair. His face was wonderfully ugly, but it was the ugliness of character, which is as attractive as beauty. His jaw and eyebrows were scraggy and rough-hewn, his nose aggressive and red-shot, his eyes small and near set, light blue in colour, and capable of assuming a very genial and also an exceedingly vindictive expression. A slight wiry moustache covered his upper lip, and his teeth were yellow, strong, and overlapping. Add to this that he seldom wore collar or necktie, that his throat was the colour and texture of the bark of a Scotch fir, and that he had a voice and especially a laugh like a bull's bellow. Then you have some idea (if you can piece all these items in your mind) of the outward James Cullingworth.

But the inner man, after all, was what was most worth noting. I don't pretend to know what genius is. Carlyle's definition always seemed to me to be a very crisp and clear statement of what it is NOT. Far from its being an infinite capacity for taking pains, its leading characteristic, as far as I have ever been able to observe it, has been that it allows the possessor of it to attain results by a sort of instinct which other men could only reach by hard work. In this sense Cullingworth was the greatest genius that I have ever known. He never seemed to work, and yet he took the anatomy prize over the heads of all the ten-hour-a-day men. That might not count for much, for he was quite capable of idling ostentatiously all day and then reading desperately all night; but start a subject of your own for him, and then see his originality and strength. Talk about torpedoes, and he would catch up a pencil, and on the back of an old envelope from his pocket he would sketch out some novel contrivance for piercing a ship's netting and getting at her side, which might no doubt involve some technical impossibility, but which would at least be quite plausible and new. Then as he drew, his bristling eyebrows would contract, his small eyes would gleam with excitement, his lips would be pressed together, and he would end by banging on the paper with his open hand, and shouting in his exultation. You would think that his one mission in life was to invent torpedoes. But next instant, if you were to express surprise as to how it was that the Egyptian workmen elevated the stones to the top of the pyramids, out would come the pencil and envelope, and he would propound a scheme for doing that with equal energy and conviction. This ingenuity was joined to an extremely sanguine nature. As he paced up and down in his jerky quick-stepping fashion after one of these flights of invention, he would take out patents for it, receive you as his partner in the enterprise, have it adopted in every civilised country, see all conceivable applications of it, count up his probable royalties, sketch out the novel methods in which he would invest his gains, and finally retire with the most gigantic fortune that has ever been amassed. And you would be swept along by his words, and would be carried every foot of the way with him, so that it would come as quite a shock to you when you suddenly fell back to earth again, and found yourself trudging the city street a poor student, with Kirk's Physiology under your arm, and hardly the price of your luncheon in your pocket.

I read over what I have written, but I can see that I give you no real insight into the demoniac cleverness of Cullingworth. His views upon medicine were most revolutionary, but I daresay that if things fulfil their promise I may have a good deal to say about them in the sequel. With his brilliant and unusual gifts, his fine athletic record, his strange way of dressing (his hat on the back of his head and his throat bare), his thundering voice, and his ugly, powerful face, he had quite the most marked individuality of any man that I have ever known.

Now, you will think me rather prolix about this man; but, as it looks as if his life might become entwined with mine, it is a subject of immediate interest to me, and I am writing all this for the purpose of reviving my own half-faded impressions, as well as in the hope of amusing and interesting you. So I must just give you one or two other points which may make his character more clear to you.

He had a dash of the heroic in him. On one occasion he was placed in such a position that he must choose between compromising a lady, or springing out of a third-floor window. Without a moment's hesitation he hurled himself out of the window. As luck would have it, he fell through a large laurel bush on to a garden plot, which was soft with rain, and so escaped with a shaking and a bruising. If I have to say anything that gives a bad impression of the man, put that upon the other side.

He was fond of rough horse-play; but it was better to avoid it with him, for you could never tell what it might lead to. His temper was nothing less than infernal. I have seen him in the dissecting-rooms begin to skylark with a fellow, and then in an instant the fun would go out of his face, his little eyes would gleam with fury, and the two would be rolling, worrying each other like dogs, below the table. He would be dragged off, panting and speechless with fury, with his wiry hair bristling straight up like a fighting terrier's.

This pugnacious side of his character would be worthily used sometimes. I remember that an address which was being given to us by an eminent London specialist was much interrupted by a man in the front row, who amused himself by interjecting remarks. The lecturer appealed to his audience at last. "These interruptions are insufferable, gentlemen," said he; "will no one free me from this annoyance?" "Hold your tongue - you, sir, on the front bench," cried culling- worth, in his bull's bellow. "Perhaps you'll make me," said the fellow, turning a contemptuous face over his shoulder. Cullingworth closed his note-book, and began to walk down on the tops of the desks to the delight of the three hundred spectators. It was fine to see the deliberate way in which he picked his way among the ink bottles. As he sprang down from the last bench on to the floor, his opponent struck him a smashing blow full in the face. Cullingworth got his bulldog grip on him, however, and rushed him backwards out of the class-room. What he did with him I don't know, but there was a noise like the delivery of a ton of coals; and the champion of law and order returned, with the sedate air of a man who had done his work. One of his eyes looked like an over-ripe damson, but we gave him three cheers as he made his way back to his seat. Then we went on with the dangers of Placenta Praevia.

He was not a man who drank hard, but a little drink would have a very great effect upon him. Then it was that the ideas would surge from his brain, each more fantastic and ingenious than the last. And if ever he did get beyond the borderland he would do the most amazing things. Sometimes it was the fighting instinct that would possess him, sometimes the preaching, and sometimes the comic, or they might come in succession, replacing each other so rapidly as to bewilder his companions. Intoxication brought all kinds of queer little peculiarities with it. One of them was that he could walk or run perfectly straight, but that there always came a time when he unconsciously returned upon his tracks and retraced his steps again. This had a strange effect sometimes, as in the instance which I am about to tell you.

Very sober to outward seeming, but in a frenzy within, he went down to the station one night, and, stooping to the pigeon-hole, he asked the ticket-clerk, in the suavest voice, whether he could tell him how far it was to London. The official put forward his face to reply when Cullingworth drove his fist through the little hole with the force of a piston. The clerk flew backwards off his stool, and his yell of pain and indignation brought some police and railway men to his assistance. They pursued Cullingworth; but he, as active and as fit as a greyhound, outraced them all, and vanished into the darkness, down the long, straight street. The pursuers had stopped, and were gathered in a knot talking the matter over, when, looking up, they saw, to their amazement, the man whom they were after, running at the top of his speed in their direction. His little peculiarity had asserted itself, you see, and he had unconsciously turned in his flight. They tripped him up, flung themselves upon him, and after a long and desperate struggle dragged him to the police station. He was charged before the magistrate next morning, but made such a brilliant speech from the dock in his own defence that he carried the Court with him, and escaped with a nominal fine. At his invitation, the witnesses and the police trooped after him to the nearest hotel, and the affair ended in universal whisky-and-sodas.

Well, now, if, after all these illustrations, I have failed to give you some notion of the man, able, magnetic, unscrupulous, interesting, many-sided, I must despair of ever doing so. I'll suppose, however, that I have not failed; and I will proceed to tell you, my most patient of confidants, something of my personal relations with Cullingworth.

When I first made a casual acquaintance with him he was a bachelor. At the end of a long vacation, however, he met me in the street, and told me, in his loud-voiced volcanic shoulder-slapping way, that he had just been married. At his invitation, I went up with him then and there to see his wife; and as we walked he told me the history of his wedding, which was as extraordinary as everything else he did. I won't tell it to you here, my dear Bertie, for I feel that I have dived down too many side streets already; but it was a most bustling business, in which the locking of a governess into her room and the dyeing of Cullingworth's hair played prominent parts. Apropos of the latter he was never quite able to get rid of its traces; and from this time forward there was added to his other peculiarities the fact that when the sunlight struck upon his hair at certain angles, it turned it all iridescent and shimmering.

Well, I went up to his lodgings with him, and was introduced to Mrs. Cullingworth. She was a timid, little, sweet-faced, grey-eyed woman, quiet-voiced and gentle-mannered. You had only to see the way in which she looked at him to understand that she was absolutely under his control, and that do what he might, or say what he might, it would always be the best thing to her. She could be obstinate, too, in a gentle, dove-like sort of way; but her obstinacy lay always in the direction of backing up his sayings and doings. This, however, I was only to find out afterwards; and at that, my first visit, she impressed me as being one of the sweetest little women that I had ever known.

They were living in the most singular style, in a suite of four small rooms, over a grocer's shop. There was a kitchen, a bedroom, a sitting-room, and a fourth room, which Cullingworth insisted upon regarding as a most unhealthy apartment and a focus of disease, though I am convinced that it was nothing more than the smell of cheeses from below which had given him the idea. At any rate, with his usual energy he had not only locked t he room up, but had gummed varnished paper over all the cracks of the door, to prevent the imaginary contagion from spreading. The furniture was the sparest possible. There were, I remember, only two chairs in the sitting-room; so that when a guest came (and I think I was the only one) Cullingworth used to squat upon a pile of yearly volumes of the British Medical Journal in the corner. I can see him now levering himself up from his lowly seat, and striding about the room roaring and striking with his hands, while his little wife sat mum in the corner, listening to him with love and admiration in her eyes. What did we care, any one of the three of us, where we sat or how we lived, when youth throbbed hot in our veins, and our souls were all aflame with the possibilities of life? I still look upon those Bohemian evenings, in the bare room amid the smell of the cheese, as being among the happiest that I have known.

I was a frequent visitor to the Cullingworths, for the pleasure that I got was made the sweeter by the pleasure which I hoped that I gave. They knew no one, and desired to know no one; so that socially I seemed to be the only link that bound them to the world. I even ventured to interfere in the details of their little menage. Cullingworth had a fad at the time, that all the diseases of civilisation were due to the abandonment of the open-air life of our ancestors, and as a corollary he kept his windows open day and night. As his wife was obviously fragile, and yet would have died before she would have uttered a word of complaint, I took it upon myself to point out to him that the cough from which she suffered was hardly to be cured so long as she spent her life in a draught. He scowled savagely at me for my interference; and I thought we were on the verge of a quarrel, but it blew over, and he became more considerate in the matter of ventilation.

Our evening occupations just about that time were of a most extraordinary character. You are aware that there is a substance, called waxy matter, which is deposited in the tissues of the body during the course of certain diseases. What this may be and how it is formed has been a cause for much bickering among pathologists. Cullingworth had strong views upon the subject, holding that the waxy matter was really the same thing as the glycogen which is normally secreted by the liver. But it is one thing to have an idea, and another to be able to prove it. Above all, we wanted some waxy matter with which to experiment. But fortune favoured us in the most magical way. The Professor of Pathology had come into possession of a magnificent specimen of the condition. With pride he exhibited the organ to us in the class-room before ordering his assistant to remove it to the ice-chest, preparatory to its being used for microscopical work in the practical class. Cullingworth saw his chance, and acted on the instant. Slipping out of the classroom, he threw open

the ice-chest, rolled his ulster round the dreadful gliste-
ning mass, closed the chest again, and walked quietly
away. I have no doubt that to this day the disappear-
ance of that waxy liver is one of the most inexplicable
mysteries in the career of our Professor.

That evening, and for many evenings to come, we
worked upon our liver. For our experiments it was
necessary to subject it all to great heat in an endeavour
to separate the nitrogenous cellular substance from the
non-nitrogenous waxy matter. With our limited applia-
nces the only way we could think of was to cut it into
fine pieces and cook it in a frying pan. So night after
night the curious spectacle might have been seen of a
beautiful young woman and two very earnest young
men busily engaged in making these grim fricassees.
Nothing came of all our work; for though Cullingworth
considered that he had absolutely established his case,
and wrote long screeds to the medical papers upon the
subject, he was never apt at stating his views with his
pen, and he left, I am sure, a very confused idea on the
minds of his readers as to what it was that he was
driving at. Again, as he was a mere student without
any letters after his name, he got scant attention, and I
never heard that he gained over a single supporter.

At the end of the year we both passed our
examinations and became duly qualified medical men.
The Cullingworths vanished away, and I never heard
any more of them, for he was a man who prided
himself upon never writing a letter. His father had
formerly a very large and lucrative practice in the West
of Scotland, but he died some years ago. I had a vague
idea, founded upon some chance remark of his, that
Cullingworth had gone to see whether the family name
might still stand him in good stead there. As for me I

began, as you will remember that I explained in my last, by acting as assistant in my father's practice. You know, however, that at its best it is not worth more than L700 a year, with no room for expansion. This is not large enough to keep two of us at work. Then, again, there are times when I can see that my religious opinions annoy the dear old man. On the whole, and for every reason, I think that it would be better if I were out of this. I applied for several steamship lines, and for at least a dozen house surgeonships; but there is as much competition for a miserable post with a hundred a year as if it were the Viceroyship of India. As a rule, I simply get my testimonials returned without any comment, which is the sort of thing that teaches a man humility. Of course, it is very pleasant to live with the mater, and my little brother Paul is a regular trump. I am teaching him boxing; and you should see him put his tiny fists up, and counter with his right. He got me under the jaw this evening, and I had to ask for poached eggs for supper.

And all this brings me up to the present time and the latest news. It is that I had a telegram from Cullingworth this morning - after nine months' silence. It was dated from Avonmouth, the town where I had suspected that he had settled, and it said simply, "Come at once. I have urgent need of you. "CULLINGWORTH." Of course, I shall go by the first train to-morrow. It may mean anything or nothing. In my heart of hearts I hope and believe that old Cullingworth sees an opening for me either as his partner or in some other way. I always believed that he would turn up trumps, and make my fortune as well as his own. He knows that if I am not very quick or brilliant I am fairly steady and reliable. So that's what I've been working up to all along, Bertie, that to-morrow I go to join Cullingworth, and that it looks as if there was to be an opening for me at last. I gave you a sketch of him and his ways, so that you may take an interest in the development of my fortune, which you could not do if you did not know something of the man who is holding out his hand to me.

Yesterday was my birthday, and I was two and twenty years of age. For two and twenty years have I swung around the sun. And in all seriousness, without a touch of levity, and from the bottom of my soul, I assure you that I have at the present moment the very vaguest idea as to whence I have come from, whither I am going, or what I am here for. It is not for want of inquiry, or from indifference. I have mastered the principles of several religions. They have all shocked me by the violence which I should have to do to my reason to accept the dogmas of any one of them. Their ethics are usually excellent. So are the ethics of the common law of England. But the scheme of creation upon which those ethics are built! Well, it really is to me the most astonishing thing that I have seen in my short earthly pilgrimage, that so many able men, deep philosophers, astute lawyers, and clear-headed men of the world should accept such an explanation of the facts of life. In the face of their apparent concurrence my own poor little opinion would not dare to do more than lurk at the back of my soul, were it not that I take courage when I reflect that the equally eminent lawyers and philosophers of Rome and Greece were all agreed that Jupiter had numerous wives and was fond of a glass of good wine.

Mind, my dear Bertie, I do not wish to run down your view or that of any other man. We who claim toleration should be the first to extend it to others. I am

Sir A. C. Doyle

only indicating my own position, as I have often done before. And I know your reply so well. Can't I hear your grave voice saying "Have faith!" Your conscience allows you to. Well, mine won't allow me. I see so clearly that faith is not a virtue, but a vice. It is a goat which has been herded with the sheep. If a man deliberately shut his physical eyes and refused to use them, you would be as quick as any one in seeing that it was immoral and a treason to Nature. And yet you would counsel a man to shut that far more precious gift, the reason, and to refuse to use it in the most intimate question of life.

"The reason cannot help in such a matter," you reply. I answer that to say so is to give up a battle before it is fought. My reason SHALL help me, and when it can help no longer I shall do without help.

It's late, Bertie, and the fire's out, and I'm shivering; and you, I'm very sure, are heartily weary of my gossip and my heresies, so adieu until my next.

II.

HOME,
10th April, 1881.

Well, my dear Bertie, here I am again in your postbox. It's not a fortnight since I wrote you that great long letter, and yet you see I have news enough to make another formidable budget. They say that the art of letter-writing has been lost; but if quantity may atone for quality, you must confess that (for your sins) you have a friend who has retained it.

When I wrote to you last I was on the eve of going down to join the Cullingworths at Avonmouth, with every hope that he had found some opening for me. I must tell you at some length the particulars of that expedition.

I travelled down part of the way with young Leslie Duncan, whom I think you know. He was gracious enough to consider that a third-class carriage and my company were to be preferred to a first class with solitude. You know that he came into his uncle's money a little time ago, and after a first delirious outbreak, he has now relapsed into that dead heavy state of despair which is caused by having everything which one can wish for. How absurd are the ambitions of life when I think that I, who am fairly happy and as keen as a razor edge, should be struggling for that which I can see has brought neither profit nor happiness to him! And yet, if I can read my own nature, it is not the accumulation of money which is my real aim, but only that I may acquire so much as will relieve my mind of sordid cares and enable me to develop any gifts which I may have, undisturbed. My tastes are so simple that I cannot imagine any advantage which wealth can give - save indeed the exquisite pleasure of helping a good man or a good cause. Why should people ever take credit for charity when they must know that they cannot gain as much pleasure out of their guineas in any other fashion? I gave my watch to a broken schoolmaster the other day (having no change in my pocket), and the mater could not quite determine whether it was a trait of madness or of nobility. I could have told her with absolute confidence that it was neither the one nor the other, but a sort of epicurean selfishness with perhaps a little dash of swagger away down at the bottom of it. What had I ever had from my chronometer like the quiet thrill of satisfaction when the fellow brought me the pawn ticket and told me that the thirty shillings had been useful?

Leslie Duncan got out at Carstairs, and I was left alone with a hale, white-haired, old Roman Catholic priest, who had sat quietly reading his office in the corner. We fell into the most intimate talk, which lasted all the way to Avonmouth - indeed, so interested was I that I very nearly passed through the place without knowing it. Father Logan (for that was his name) seemed to me to be a beautiful type of what a priest should be - self-sacrificing and pure-minded, with a kind of simple cunning about him, and a deal of innocent fun. He had the defects as well as the virtues of his class, for he was absolutely reactionary in his views. We discussed religion with fervour, and his theology was somewhere about the Early Pliocene. He might have chattered the matter over with a priest of Charlemagne's Court, and they would have shaken hands after every sentence. He would acknowledge this and claim it as a merit. It was consistency in his eyes. If our astronomers and inventors and law-givers had been equally consistent where would modern civilisation be? Is religion the only domain of thought which is non-progressive, and to be referred for ever to a standard set two thousand years ago? Can they not see that as the human brain evolves it must take a wider outlook? A half-formed brain makes a half-formed God, and who shall say that our brains are even half-formed yet? The truly inspired priest is the man or woman with the big brain. It is not the shaven patch on the outside, but it is the sixty ounces within which is the real mark of election.

You know that you are turning up your nose at me, Bertie. I can see you do it. But I'll come off the thin ice, and you shall have nothing but facts now. I'm afraid that I should never do for a story-teller, for the first stray character that comes along puts his arm in mine and walks me off, with my poor story straggling away to nothing behind me.

Well, then, it was night when we reached Avonmouth, and as I popped my head out of the carriage window, the first thing that my eyes rested upon was old Cullingworth, standing in, the circle of light under agas-lamp. His frock coat was flying open, his waistcoat unbuttoned at the top, and his hat (a top hat this time) jammed on the back of his head, with his bristling hair spurting out in front of it. In every way, save that he wore a collar, he was the same Cullingworth as ever. He gave a roar of recognition when he saw me, bustled me out of my carriage, seized

Sir A. C. Doyle

my carpet bag, or grip-sack as you used to call it, and a minute later we were striding along together through the streets.

I was, as you may imagine, all in a tingle to know what it was that he wanted with me. However, as he made no allusion to it, I did not care to ask, and, during our longish walk, we talked about indifferent matters. It was football first, I remember, whether Richmond had a chance against Blackheath, and the way in which the new passing game was shredding the old scrimmages. Then he got on to inventions, and became so excited that he had to give me back my bag in order that he might be able to slap all his points home with his fist upon his palm. I can see him now stopping, with his face leaning forward and his yellow tusks gleaming in the lamplight.

"My dear Munro" (this was the style of the thing), "why was armour abandoned, eh? What! I'll tell you why. It was because the weight of metal that would protect a man who was standing up was more than he could carry. But battles are not fought now-a-days by men who are standing up. Your infantry are all lying on their stomachs, and it would take very little to protect them. And steel has improved, Munro! Chilled steel! Bessemer! Bessemer! Very good. How much to cover a man? Fourteen inches by twelve, meeting at an angle so that the bullet will glance. A notch at one side for the rifle. There you have it, laddie - the Culling-worth patent portable bullet-proof shield! Weight? Oh, the weight would be sixteen pounds. I worked it out. Each company carries its shields in go-carts, and they are served out on going into action. Give me twenty thousand good shots, and I'll go in at Calais and come out at Pekin. Think of it, my boy! the moral effect. One side gets home every time and the other plasters its bullets up against steel plates. No troops would stand it. The nation that gets it first will pitchfork the rest of Europe over the edge. They're bound to have it - all of them. Let's reckon it out. There's about eight million of them on a war footing. Let us suppose that only half of them have it. I say only half, because I don't want to be too sanguine. That's four million, and I should take a royalty of four shillings on wholesale orders. What's that, Munro? About three-quarters of a million sterling, eh? How's that, laddie, eh? What?"

Really, that is not unlike his style of talk, now that I come to read it over, only you miss the queer stops, the sudden confidential whispers, the roar with which he triumphantly answered his own questions, the shrugs and slaps, and gesticulations. But not a word all the time as to what it was that made him send me that urgent wire which brought me to Avonmouth.

I had, of course, been puzzling in my mind as to whether he had succeeded or not, though from his cheerful appearance and buoyant talk, it was tolerably clear to me that all was well with him. I was, however, surprised when, as we walked along a quiet, curving avenue, with great houses standing in their own grounds upon either side, he stopped and turned in through the iron gate which led up to one of the finest of them. The moon had broken out and shone upon the high-peaked roof, and upon the gables at each corner. When he knocked it was opened by a footman with red plush knee-breeches. I began to perceive that my friend's success must have been something colossal.

When we came down to the dining-room for supper, Mrs.Cullingworth was waiting there to greet me. I was sorry to see that she was pale and weary-looking. However, we had a merry meal in the old style, and her husband's animation reflected itself upon her face, until at last we might have been back in the little room, where the Medical Journals served as a chair, instead of in the great oak-furnished, picture-hung chamber to which we had been promoted. All the time, however, not one word as to the object of my journey.

When the supper was finished, Cullingworth led the way into a small sitting-room, where we both lit our pipes, and Mrs. Cullingworth her cigarette. He sat for some little time in silence, and then bounding up rushed to the door and flung it open. It is always one of his strange peculiarities to think that people are eavesdropping or conspiring against him; for, in spite of his superficial brusqueness and frankness, a strange vein of suspicion runs through his singular and complex nature. Having satisfied himself now that there were no spies or listeners he threw himself down into his armchair.

"Munro," said he, prodding at me with his pipe, "what I wanted to tell you is, that I am utterly, hopelessly, and irretrievably ruined."

My chair was tilted on its back legs as he spoke, and I assure you that I was within an ace of going over. Down like a pack of cards came all my dreams as to the grand results which were to spring from my journey to Avonmouth. Yes, Bertie, I am bound to confess it: my first thought was of my own disappointment, and my second of the misfortune of my friends. He had the most diabolical intuitions, or I a very telltale face, for he added at once -

"Sorry to disappoint you, my boy. That's not what you expected to hear, I can see."

"Well," I stammered, "it IS rather a surprise, old chap. I thought from the . . . from the . . ."

"From the house, and the footman, and the furniture," said he. "Well, they've eaten me up among them . . . licked me clean, bones and gravy. I'm done for, my boy, unless . . ." - here I saw a question in his eyes - "unless some friend were to lend me his name on a bit of stamped paper."

"I can't do it, Cullingworth," said I." It's a wretched thing to have to refuse a friend; and if I had money . . ."

"Wait till you're asked, Munro," he interrupted, with his ugliest of expressions. "Besides, as you have nothing and no prospects, what earthly use would YOUR name on a paper be?"

"That's what I want to know," said I, feeling a little mortified, none the less.

"Look here, laddie," he went on; "d'you see that pile of letters on the left of the table?"

"Yes."

"Those are duns. And d'you see those documents on the right? Well, those are County Court summonses. And, now, d'you see that;" he picked up a little ledger, and showed me three or, four names scribbled on the first page.

Sir A. C. Doyle

"That's the practice," he roared, and laughed until the great veins jumped out on his forehead. His wife laughed heartily also, just as she would have wept, had he been so disposed.

"It's this way, Munro," said he, when he had got over his paroxysm. "You have probably heard - in fact, I have told you myself - that my father had the finest practice in Scotland. As far as I could judge he was a man of no capacity, but still there you are - he had it."

I nodded and smoked.

"Well, he's been dead seven years, and fifty nets dipping into his little fish-pond. However, when I passed I thought my best move was to come down to the old place, and see whether I couldn't piece the thing together again. The name ought to be worth something, I thought. But it was no use doing the thing in a half hearted way. Not a bit of use in that, Munro. The kind of people who came to him were wealthy, and must see a fine house and a man in livery. What chance was there of gathering them into a bow-windowed forty pound-a-year house with a grubby-faced maid at the door? What do you suppose I did? My boy, I took the governor's old house, that was unlet - the very house that he kept up at five thousand a year. Off I started in rare style, and sank my last cent in furniture. But it's no use, laddie. I can't hold on any longer. I got two accidents and an epileptic - twenty-two pounds, eight and sixpence - that's the lot!

"What will you do, then?"

"That's what I wanted your advice about. That's why I wired for you. I always respected your opinion, my boy, and I thought that now was the time to have it."

It struck me that if he had asked for it nine months before there would have been more sense in it. What on earth could I do when affairs were in such a tangle? However, I could not help feeling complimented when so independent a fellow as Cullingworth turned to me in this way.

"You really think," said I, "that it is no use holding on here?"

He jumped up, and began pacing the room in his swift jerky way.

"You take warning from it, Munro," said he. "You've got to start yet. Take my tip, and go where no one knows you. People will trust a stranger quick enough; but if they can remember you as a little chap who ran about in knickerbockers, and got spanked with a hair brush for stealing plums, they are not going to put their lives in your keeping. It's all very well to talk about friendship and family connections; but when a man has a pain in the stomach he doesn't care a toss about all that. I'd stick it up in gold, letters in every medical class-room - have it carved across the gate of the University - that if a man wants friends be must go among strangers. It's all up here, Munro; so there's no use in advising me to hold on."

I asked him how much he owed. It came to about seven hundred pounds. The rent alone was two hundred. He had already raised money on the furniture, and his whole assets came to less than a tenner. Of course, there was only one possible thing that I could advise.

"You must call your creditors together," said I; "they can see for themselves that you are young and energetic - sure to succeed sooner or later. If they push you into a corner now, they can get nothing. Make that clear to them. But if you make a fresh start elsewhere and succeed, you may pay them all in full. I see no other possible way out of it."

"I knew that you'd say that, and it's just what I thought myself. Isn't it, Hetty? Well, then, that settles it; and I am much obliged to you for your advice, and that's all we'll say about the matter to-night. I've made my shot and missed. Next time I shall hit, and it won't be long either."

His failure did not seem to weigh very heavily on his mind, for in a few minutes he was shouting away as lustily as ever. Whiskey and hot water were brought in, that we might all drink luck to the second venture.

And this whiskey led us to what might have been a troublesome affair. Cullingworth, who had drunk off a couple of glasses, waited until his wife had left the room, and then began to talk of the difficulty of getting any exercise now that he had to wait in all day in the hope of patients. This led us round to the ways in which a man might take his exercise indoors, and that to boxing. Cullingworth took a couple of pairs of gloves out of a cupboard, and proposed that we should fight a round or two then and there.

If I hadn't been a fool, Bertie, I should never have consented. It's one of my many weaknesses, that, whether it's a woman or a man, anything like a challenge sets me off. But I knew Cullingworth's ways, and I told you in my last what a lamb of a temper he has. None the less, we pushed back the table, put the lamp on a high bracket, and stood up to one another.

The moment I looked him in the face I smelled mischief. He had a gleam of settled malice in his eye. I believe it was my refusal to back his paper which was running in his head. Anyway he looked as dangerous as he could look, with his scowling face sunk forward a little, his hands down near his hips (for his boxing, like everything else about him, is unconventional), and his jaw set like a rat-trap.

I led off, and then in he came hitting with both hands, and grunting like a pig at every blow. From what I could see of him he was no boxer at all, but just a formidable rough and tumble fighter. I was guarding with both hands for half a minute, and then was rushed clean off my legs and banged up against the door, with my head nearly through one of the panels. He wouldn't stop then, though he saw that I had no space to get my elbows back; and he let fly a right-hander which would have put me into the hall, if I hadn't slipped it and got back to the middle of the room.

"Look here, Cullingworth," said I; "there's not much boxing about this game."

"Yes, I hit pretty hard, don't I?"

"If you come boring into me like that, I'm bound to hit you out again," I said. "I want to play light if you'll let me."

The words were not out of my mouth before he was on me like a flash. I slipped him again; but the room was so small, and he as active as a cat, that there was no getting away from him. He was on me once more with a regular football rush that knocked me off my balance. Before I knew where I was he got his left on the mark and his right on my ear. I tripped over a footstool, and then before I could get my balance he had me on the same ear again, and my head was singing like a tea-kettle. He was as pleased as possible with himself, blowing out his chest and slapping it with his palms as he took his place in the middle of the room.

"Say when you've had enough, Munro," said he.

This was pretty stiff, considering that I had two inches the better of him in height, and as many stone in weight, besides being the better boxer. His energy and the size of the room had been against me so far, but he wasn't to have all the slogging to himself in the next round if I could help it.

In he came with one of his windmill rushes. But I was on the look-out for him this time. I landed him with my left a regular nose-ender as he came, and then, ducking under his left, I got him a cross-counter on the jaw that laid him flat across his own hearthrug. He was up in an instant, with a face like a madman.

"You swine!" he shouted. "Take those gloves off, and put your hands up!" He was tugging at his own to get them off.

"Go on, you silly ass!" said I. "What is there to fight about?"

He was mad with passion, and chucked his gloves down under the table.

"By God, Munro," he cried, "if you don't take those gloves off, I'll go for you, whether you have them on or not."

"Have a glass of soda water," said I.

He made a crack at me. "You're afraid of me, Munro. That's what's the matter with you," he snarled.

This was getting too hot, Bertie. I saw all the folly of the thing. I believed that I might whip him; but at the same time I knew that we were so much of a match that we would both get pretty badly cut up without any possible object to serve. For all that, I took my gloves off, and I think perhaps it was the wisest course after all. If Cullingworth once thought he had the whiphand of you, you might be sorry for it afterwards.

But, as fate would have it, our little barney was nipped in the bud. Mrs. Cullingworth came into the room at that instant, and screamed out when she saw her husband. His nose was bleeding and his chin was all slobbered with blood, so that I don't wonder that it gave her a turn.

"James!" she screamed; and then to me": "What is the meaning of this, Mr. Munro?"

You should have seen the hatred in her dove's eyes. I felt an insane impulse to pick her up and kiss her.

"We've only been having a little spar, Mrs. Cullingworth," said I. "Your husband was complaining that he never got any exercise."

"It's all right, Hetty," said he, pulling his coat on again.

"Don't be a little stupid. Are the servants gone to bed? Well, you might bring some water in a basin from the kitchen. Sit down, Munro, and light your pipe again. I have a hundred things that I want to talk to you about."

So that was the end of it, and all went smoothly for the rest of the evening. But, for all that, the little wife will always look upon me as a brute and a bully; while as to Cullingworth -- well, it's rather difficult to say what Cullingworth thinks about the matter.

When I woke next morning he was in my room, and a funny-looking object he was. His dressing-gown lay on a chair, and he was putting up a fifty-six pound dumb-bell, without a rag to cover him. Nature didn't give him a very symmetrical face, nor the sweetest of expressions; but he has a figure like a Greek statue. I was amused to see that both his eyes had a touch of shadow to them. It was his turn to grin when I sat up and found that my ear was about the shape and consistence of a toadstool. However, he was all for peace that morning, and chatted away in the most amiable manner possible.

I was to go back to my father's that day, but I had a couple of hours with Cullingworth in his consulting room before I left. He was in his best form, and full of a hundred fantastic schemes, by which I was to help him. His great object was to get his name into the newspapers. That was the basis of all success, according to his views. It seemed to me that he was confounding cause with effect; but I did not argue the point. I laughed until my sides ached over the grotesque suggestions which poured from him. I was to lie senseless in the roadway, and to be carried into him by a sympathising crowd, while the footman ran with a paragraph to the newspapers. But there was the likelihood that the crowd might carry me in to the rival practitioner opposite. In various disguises I was to feign fits at his very door, and so furnish fresh copy for the local press. Then I was to die - absolutely to expire - and all Scotland was to resound with how Dr. Cullingworth, of Avonmouth, had resuscitated me. His ingenious brain rang a thousand changes out of the idea, and his own impending bankruptcy was crowded right out of his thoughts by the flood of half-serious devices.

But the thing that took the fun out of him, and made him gnash his teeth, and stride cursing about the room, was to see a patient walking up the steps which led to the door of Scarsdale, his opposite neighbour. Scarsdale had a fairly busy practice, and received his people at home from ten to twelve, so that I got quite used to seeing Cullingworth fly out of his chair, and rush raving to the window. He would diagnose the cases, too, and estimate their money value until he was hardly articulate.

"There you are!" he would suddenly yell; "see that man with a limp! Every morning he goes. Displaced semilunar cartilage, and a three months' job. The man's worth thirty-five shillings a week. And there! I'm hanged if the woman with the rheumatic arthritis isn't round in her bath-chair again. She's all sealskin and lactic acid. It's simply sickening to see how they crowd to that man. And such a man! You haven't seen him. All the better for you. I don't know what the devil you are laughing at, Munro. I can't see where the fun comes in myself."

Well, it was a short experience that visit to Avonmouth, but I think that I shall remember it all my life.

Sir A. C. Doyle

Goodness knows, you must be sick enough of the subject, but when I started with so much detail I was tempted to go. It ended by my going back again in the afternoon, Cullingworth assuring me that he would call his creditors together as I had advised, and that he would let me know the result in a few days. Mrs. C. would hardly shake hands with me when I said goodbye; but I like her the better for that. He must have a great deal of good in him, or he could not have won her love and confidence so completely. Perhaps there is another Cullingworth behind the scenes - a softer, tenderer man, who can love and invite love. If there is, I have never got near him. And yet I may only have been tapping at the shell. Who knows? For that matter, it is likely enough that he has never got at the real Johnnie Munro. But you have, Bertie; and I think that you've had a little too much of him this time, only you encourage me to this sort of excess by your sympathetic replies. Well, I've done as much as the General Post Office will carry for fivepence, so I'll conclude by merely remarking that a fortnight has passed, and that I have had no news from Avonmouth, which does not in the very slightest degree surprise me. If I ever do hear anything, which is exceedingly doubtful, you may be sure that I will put a finish to this long story.

III.

HOME,
15th October, 1881.

Without any figure of speech I feel quite ashamed when I think of you, Bertie. I send you one or two enormously long letters, burdened, as far as I can remember them, with all sorts of useless detail. Then, in spite of your kindly answers and your sympathy, which I have done so little to deserve, I drop you completely for more than six months. By this J pen I swear that it shall not happen again; and this letter may serve to bridge the gap and to bring you up to date in my poor affairs, in which, of all outer mankind, you alone take an interest.

To commence with what is of most moment, you may rest assured that what you said in your last letter about religion has had my most earnest attention. I am sorry that I have not got it by me to refer to (I lent it to Charlie), but I think I have the contents in my head. It is notorious, as you say, that an unbeliever may be as bigoted as any of the orthodox, and that a man may be very dogmatic in his opposition to dogma. Such men are the real enemies of free thought. If anything could persuade me to turn traitor to my reason, it would, for example, be the blasphemous and foolish pictures displayed in some of the agnostic journals.

But every movement has its crowd of camp followers. who straggle and scatter. We are like a comet, bright at the head but tailing away into mere gas behind. However, every man may speak for himself, and I do not feel that your charge comes home to me. I am only bigoted against bigotry, and that I hold to be as legitimate as violence to the violent. When one considers what effect the perversion of the religious instinct has had during the history of the world; the bitter wars, Christian and Mahomedan, Catholic and Protestant; the persecutions, the torturings, the domestic hatreds, the petty spites, with ALL creeds equally blood-guilty, one cannot but be amazed that the concurrent voice of mankind has not placed bigotry at the very head of the deadly sins. It is surely a truism to say that neither smallpox nor the plague have brought the same misery upon mankind.

I cannot be bigoted, my dear boy, when I say from the bottom of my heart that I respect every good Catholic and every good Protestant, and that I recognise that each of these forms of faith has been a powerful instrument in the hands of that inscrutable Providence which rules all things. Just as in the course of history one finds that the most far-reaching and admirable effects may proceed from a crime; so in religion, although a creed be founded upon an entirely inadequate conception of the Creator and His ways, it may none the less be the very best practical thing for the people and age which have adopted it. But if it is right for those to whom it is intellectually satisfying to adopt it, it is equally so for those to whom it is not, to protest against it, until by this process the whole mass of mankind gets gradually leavened, and pushed a little further upon their slow upward journey.

Catholicism is the more thorough. Protestantism is the more reasonable. Protestantism adapts itself to modern civilisation. Catholicism expects civilisation to adapt itself to it. Folk climb from the one big branch to the other big branch, and think they have made a prodigious change, when the main trunk is rotten beneath them, and both must in their present forms be involved sooner or later in a common ruin. The movement of human thought, though slow, is still in the direction of truth, and the various religions which man sheds as he advances (each admirable in its day) will serve, like buoys dropped down from a sailing vessel, to give the rate and direction of his progress.

But how do I know what is truth, you ask? I don't. But I know particularly well what isn't. And surely that is something to have gained. It isn't true that the great central Mind that planned all things is capable of jealousy or of revenge, or of cruelty or of injustice. These are human attributes; and the book which ascribes them to the Infinite must be human also. It isn't true that the laws of Nature have been capriciously disturbed, that snakes have talked, that women have been turned to salt, that rods have brought water out of rocks. You must in honesty confess that if these things were presented to us when we were, adults for the first time, we should smile at them. It isn't true that the Fountain of all common sense should punish a race for a venial offence committed by a person long since dead, and then should add to the crass injustice by heaping the whole retribution upon a single innocent scapegoat. Can you not see all the want of justice and logic, to say nothing of the want of mercy, involved in such a conception? Can you not see it, Bertie? How can you blind yourself to it! Take your eyes away from the details for a moment, and look at this root idea of the predominant Faith. Is the general conception of it consistent with infinite wisdom and mercy? If not, what becomes of the dogmas, the sacraments, the whole scheme which is founded upon this sand-bank? Courage, my friend! At the right moment all will be laid aside, as the man whose strength increases lays down the crutch which has been a good friend to him in his weakness. But his changes won't be over then. His hobble will become a walk, and his walk a run. There is no finality - CAN be none since the question concerns the infinite. All this, which appears too advanced to you to-day, will seem reactionary and conservative a thousand years hence.

Since I am upon this topic, may I say just a little more without boring you? You say that criticism such as mine is merely destructive, and that I have nothing to offer in place of what I pull down. This is not quite correct. I think that there are certain elemental truths within our grasp which ask for no faith for their acceptance, and which are sufficient to furnish us with a practical religion, having so much of reason in it that it would draw thinking men into its fold, not drive them forth from it.

When we all get back to these elemental and provable facts there will be some hopes of ending the petty bickerings of creeds, and of including the whole human family in one comprehensive system of thought.

When fir t I came out of the faith in which I had been reared, I certainly did feel for a time as if my life-belt had burst. I won't exaggerate and say that I was miserable and plunged in utter spiritual darkness. Youth is too full of action for that. But I was conscious of a vague unrest, of a constant want of repose, of an emptiness and hardness which I had not noticed in life before. I had so identified religion with the Bible that I could not conceive them apart. When the foundation proved false, the whole structure came rattling about my ears. And then good old Carlyle came to the rescue; and partly from him, and partly from my own broodings, I made a little hut of my own, which has kept me snug ever since, and has even served to shelter a friend or two besides.

The first and main thing was to get it thoroughly soaked into one that the existence of a Creator and an indication of His attributes does in no way depend upon Jewish poets, nor upon human paper or printing ink. On the contrary, all such efforts to realise Him must only belittle Him, bringing the Infinite down to the narrow terms of human thought, at a time when that thought was in the main less spiritual than it is at present. Even the most material of modern minds would flinch at depicting the Deity as ordering wholesale executions, and hacking kings to pieces upon the horns of altars.

Then having prepared your mind for a higher (if perhaps a vaguer) idea of the Deity, proceed to study Him in His works, which cannot be counterfeited or manipulated. Nature is the true revelation of the Deity to man. The nearest green field is the inspired page from which you may read all that it is needful for you to know.

I confess that I have never been able to understand the position of the atheist. In fact, I have come to disbelieve in his existence, and to look upon the word as a mere term of theological reproach. It may represent a temporary condition, a passing mental phase, a defiant reaction against an anthropomorphic ideal; but I cannot conceive that any man can continue to survey Nature and to deny that there are laws at work which display intelligence and power. The very existence of a world carries with it the proof of a world-maker, as the table guarantees the pre-existence of the carpenter. Granting this, one may form what conception one will of that Maker, but one cannot be an atheist.

Wisdom and power and means directed to an end run all through the scheme of Nature. What proof do we want, then, from a book? If the man who observes the myriad stars, and considers that they and their innumerable satellites move in their serene dignity through the heavens, each swinging clear of the other's orbit - if, I say, the man who sees this cannot realise the Creator's attributes without the help of the book of Job, then his view of things is beyond my under-standing. Nor is it only in the large things that we see the ever present solicitude of some intelligent force. Nothing is too tiny for that fostering care. We see the minute proboscis of the insect carefully adjusted to fit into the calyx of the flower, the most microscopic hair and gland each with its definite purposeful function to perform. What matter whether these came by special creation or by evolution? We know as a matter of fact that they came by evolution, but that only defines the law. It does not explain it.

But if this power has cared for the bee so as to furnish it with its honey bag and its collecting forceps, and for the lowly seed so as to have a thousand devices by which it reaches a congenial soil, then is it conceivable that we, the highest product of all, are overlooked? It is

NOT conceivable. The idea is inconsistent with the scheme of creation as we see it. I say again that no faith is needed to attain the certainty of a most watchful Providence.

And with this certainty surely we have all that is necessary for an elemental religion. Come what may after death, our duties lie clearly defined before us in this life; and the ethical standard of all creeds agrees so far that there is not likely to be any difference of opinion as to that. The last reformation simplified Catholicism. The coming one will simplify Protestantism. And when the world is ripe for it another will come and simplify that. The ever improving brain will give us an ever broadening creed. Is it not glorious to think that evolution is still living and acting - that if we have an anthropoid ape as an ancestor, we may have archangels for our posterity?

Well, I really never intended to inflict all this upon you, Bertie. I thought I could have made my position clear in a page or so. But you can see how one point has brought up another. Even now I am leaving so much unsaid. I can see with such certainty exactly what you will say. "If you deduce a good Providence from the good things in nature, what do you make of the evil?" That's what you will say. Suffice it that I am inclined to deny the existence of evil. Not another word will I say upon the subject; but if you come back to it yourself, then be it on your own head.

You remember that when I wrote last I had just returned from visiting the Cullingworths at Avonmouth, and that he had promised to let me know what steps he took in appeasing his creditors. As I expected, I have not had one word from him since. But in a roundabout way I did get some news as to what happened. From this account, which was second-hand, and may have been exaggerated, Cullingworth did exactly what I had recommended, and calling all his creditors together he made them a long statement as to his position. The good people were so touched by the picture that he drew of a worthy man fighting against adversity that several of them wept, and there was not only complete unanimity as to letting their bills stand over, but even some talk of a collection then and there to help Cullingworth on his way. He has, I understand, left Avonmouth, but no one has any idea what has become of him. It is generally supposed that he has gone to England. He is a strange fellow, but I wish him luck wherever he goes.

When I came back I settled down once more to the routine of my father's practice, holding on there until something may turn up. And for six months I have had to wait; a weary six months they have been. You see I cannot ask my father for money - or, at least, I cannot bring myself to take an unnecessary penny of his money - for I know how hard a fight it is with him to keep the roof over our heads and pay for the modest little horse and trap which are as necessary to his trade as a goose is to a tailor. Foul fare the grasping taxman who wrings a couple of guineas from us on the plea that it is a luxury! We can just hold on, and I would not have him a pound the poorer for me. But you can understand, Bertie, that it is humiliating for a man of my age to have to go about without any money in my pocket. It affects me in so many petty ways. A poor man may do me a kindness, and I have to seem mean in his eyes. I may want a flower for a girl, and must be content to appear ungallant. I don't know why I should be ashamed of this, since it is no fault of mine, and I hope that I don't show it to any one else that I AM ashamed of it; but to you, my dear Bertie, I don't mind confessing that it hurts my self-respect terribly.

I have often wondered why some of those writing fellows don't try their hands at drawing the inner life of a young man from about the age of puberty until he begins to find his feet a little. Men are very fond of analysing the feelings of their heroines, which they cannot possibly know anything about, while they have little to say of the inner development of their heroes, which is an experience which they have themselves undergone. I should like to try it myself, but it would need blending with fiction, and I never had a spark of imagination. But I have a vivid recollection of what I went through myself. At the time I thought (as everybody thinks) that it was a unique experience; but since I have heard the confidences of my father's patients I am convinced that it is the common lot. The shrinking, horrible shyness, alternating with occasional absurd fits of audacity which represent the reaction against it, the longing for close friendship, the agonies over imaginary slights, the extraordinary sexual doubts, the deadly fears caused by non-existent diseases, the vague emotion produced by all women, and the half-frightened thrill by particular ones, the aggressiveness caused by fear of being afraid, the sudden blacknesses, the profound self-distrust - I dare bet that you have felt every one of them, Bertie, just as I have, and that the first lad of eighteen whom you see out of your window is suffering from them now.

This is all a digression, however, from the fact that I have been six months at home and am weary of it, and pleased at the new development of which I shall have to tell you. The practice here, although unremunerative, is very busy with its three-and-sixpenny visits and guinea confinements, so that both the governor and I have had plenty to do. You know how I admire him, and yet I fear there is little intellectual sympathy between us. He appears to think that those opinions of mine upon religion and politics which come hot from my inmost soul have been assumed either out of indiff- erence or bravado. So I have ceased to talk on vital subjects with him, and, though we affect to ignore it, we both know that there is a barrier there. Now, with my mother - ah, but my mother must have a paragraph to herself.

You met her, Bertie! You must remember her sweet face, her sensitive mouth, her peering, short-sighted eyes, her general suggestion of a plump little hen, who is still on the alert about her chickens. But you cannot realise all that she is to me in our domestic life. Those helpful fingers! That sympathetic brain! Ever since I can remember her she has been the quaintest mixture of the housewife and the woman of letters, with the highbred spirited lady as a basis for either character. Always a lady, whether she was bargaining with the butcher, or breaking in a skittish charwoman, or stirring the porridge, which I can see her doing with the porridge-stick in one hand, and the other holding her Revue des deux Mondes within two inches of her dear nose. That was always her favourite reading, and I can never think of her without the association of its browny-yellow cover.

She is a very well-read woman is the mother; she keeps up to date in French literature as well as in English, and can talk by the hour about the Goncourts, and Flaubert, and Gautier. Yet she is always hard at work; and how she imbibes all her knowledge is a mystery. She reads when she knits, she reads when she scrubs, she even reads when she feeds her babies. We have a little joke against her, that at an interesting passage she deposited a spoonful of rusk and milk into my little sister's car-hole, the child having turned her head at the critical instant. Her hands are worn with work, and yet where is the idle woman who has read as much?

Then, there is her family pride. That is a very vital portion of the mother. You know how little I think of such things. If the Esquire were to be snipped once and for ever from the tail of my name I should be the lighter for it. But, ma foi! - to use her own favourite expletive - it would not do to say this to her. On the Packenham side (she is a Packenham) the family can boast of some fairly good men - I mean on the direct line - but when we get on the side branches there is not a monarch upon earth who does not roost on that huge family tree. Not once, nor twice, but thrice did the Plantagenets intermarry with us, the Dukes of Brittany courted our alliance, and the Percies of Northumberland intertwined themselves with our whole illustrious record. So in my boyhood she would expound the matter, with hearthbrush in one hand and a glove full of cinders in the other, while I would sit swinging my knickerbockered legs, swelling with pride until my waistcoat was as tight as a sausage skin, as I contemplated the gulf which separated me from all other little boys who swang their legs upon tables. To this day if I chance to do anything of which she strongly approves, the dear heart can say no more than that I am a thorough Packenham; while if I fall away from the straight path, she says with a sigh that there are points in which I take after the Munros.

She is broad-minded and intensely practical in her ordinary moods, though open to attacks of romance. I can recollect her coming to see me at a junction through which my train passed, with a six months' absence on either side of the incident. We had five minutes' conversation, my head out of the carriage window. "Wear flannel next your skin, my dear boy, and never believe in eternal punishment," was her last item of advice as we rolled out of the station. Then to finish her portrait I need not tell you, who have seen her, that she is young-looking and comely to be the mother of about thirty-five feet of humanity. She was in the railway carriage and I on the platform the other day. "Your husband had better get in or we'll go without him," said the guard. As we went off, the mother was fumbling furiously in her pocket, and I know that she was looking for a shilling.

Ah! what a gossip I have been! And all to lead up to the one sentence that I could not have stayed at home this six months if it had not been for the company and the sympathy of my mother.

Well, now I want to tell you about the scrape that I got myself into. I suppose that I ought to pull a long face over it, but for the life of me I can't help laughing. I have you almost up to date in my history now, for what I am going to tell you happened only last week. I must mention no names here even to you; for the curse of Ernulphus, which includes eight and forty minor imprecations, be upon the head of the man who kisses and tells.

You must know, then, that within the boundaries of this city there are two ladies, a mother and a daughter, whom I shall call Mrs. and Miss Laura Andrews. They are patients of the governor's, and have become to some extent friends of the family. Madame is Welsh, charming in appearance, dignified in her manners, and High Church in her convictions. The daughter is rather taller than the mother, but otherwise they are strikingly alike. The mother is thirty-six and the daughter eighteen. Both are exceedingly charming. Had I to choose between them, I think, entrenous, that the mother would have attracted me most, for I am thoroughly of Balzac's opinion as to the woman of thirty. However, fate was to will it otherwise.

It was the coming home from a dance which first brought Laura and me together. You know how easily and suddenly these things happen, beginning in playful teasing and ending in something a little warmer than friendship. You squeeze the slender arm which is passed through yours, you venture to take the little gloved hand, you say good night at absurd length in the shadow of the door. It is innocent and very interesting, love trying his wings in a first little flutter. He will keep his sustained flight later on, the better for the practice. There was never any question of engagements between us, nor any suggestion of harm. She knew that I was a poor devil with neither means nor prospects, and I knew that her mother's will was her law, and that her course was already marked out for her. However, we exchanged our little confidences, and met occasionally by appointment, and tried to make our lives brighter without darkening those of any one else. I can see you shake your head here and growl, like the comfortable married man that you are, that such relations are very dangerous. So they are, my boy: but neither of us cared, she out of innocence and I out of recklessness, for from the beginning all the fault in the matter was mine.

Well, matters were in this state when one day last week a note came up to the Dad saying that Mrs. Andrews' servant was ill, and would he come at once. The old man had a touch of gout, so I donned my professional coat and sallied forth, thinking that perhaps I might combine pleasure with business, and have a few words with Laura. Sure enough, as I passed up the gravel drive which curves round to the door, I glanced through the drawing-room window, and saw her sitting painting, with her back to the light. It was clear that she had not heard me. The hall door was ajar, and when I pushed it open, no one was in the hall. A sudden fit of roguishness came over me. I pushed the drawing-room door very slowly wider, crept in on tiptoe, stole quietly across, and bending down, I kissed the artist upon the nape of her neck. She turned round with a squeal, and it was the mother!

I don't know whether you have ever been in a tighter corner than that, Bertie. It was quite tight enough for me. I remember that I smiled as I stole across the carpet on that insane venture. I did not smile again that evening. It makes me hot now when I think of it.

Well, I made the most dreadful fool of myself. At first, the good lady who (as I think I told you) is very dignified and rather reserved, could not believe her senses. Then, as the full force of my enormity came upon her she reared herself up until she seemed the tallest and the coldest woman I had ever seen. It was an interview with a refrigerator. She asked me what I had ever observed in her conduct which had encourag- ed me to subject her to such an outrage. I saw, of course, that any excuses upon my part would put her on the right track and give poor Laura away; so I stood with my hair bristling and my top hat in my hand, presenting, I am sure, a most extraordinary figure. Indeed, she looked rather funny herself, with her palette in one hand, her brush in the other, and the blank astonishment on her face. I stammered out something about hoping that she did not mind, which made her more angry than ever. "The only possible excuse for your conduct, sir, is that you are under the influence of drink," said she. "I need not say that we do not require the services of a medical man in that condition." I did not try to disabuse her of the idea, for really I could see no better explanation; so I beat a retreat in a very demoralised condition. She wrote a letter to my father about it in the evening, and the old man was very angry indeed. As to the mother, she is as staunch as steel, and quite prepared to prove that poor Mrs. A. was a very deep designing person, who had laid a trap for innocent Johnnie. So there has been a grand row; and not a soul upon earth has the least idea of what it all means, except only yourself as you read this letter.

You can imagine that this has not contributed to make life here more pleasant, for my father cannot bring himself to forgive me. Of course, I don't wonder at his anger. I should be just the same myself. It does look like a shocking breach of professional honour, and a sad disregard of his interests. If he knew the truth he would see that it was nothing worse than a silly ill-timed boyish joke. However, he never shall know the truth.

And now there is some chance of my getting something to do. We had a letter to-night from Christie & Howden, the writers to the Signet, saying that they desire an interview with me, in view of a possible appointment. We can't imagine what it means, but I am full of hopes. I go to-morrow morning to see them, and I shall let you know the result.

Good-bye, my dear Bertie! Your life flows in a steady stream, and mine in a broken torrent. Yet I would have every detail of what happens to you.

IV.

HOME,
1st December, 1881.

I may be doing you an injustice, Bertie, but it seemed
to me in your last that there were indications that the
free expression of my religious views had been
distasteful to you. That you should disagree with me I
am prepared for; but that you should object to free and
honest discussion of those subjects which above all
others men should be honest over, would, I confess, be
a disappointment. The Freethinker is placed at this
disadvantage in ordinary society, that whereas it would
be considered very bad taste upon his part to obtrude
his unorthodox opinion, no such consideration hampers
those with whom he disagrees. There was a time when
it took a brave man to be a Christian. Now it takes a
brave man not to be. But if we are to wear a gag, and
hide our thoughts when writing in confidence to our
most intimate -- no, but I won't believe it. You and I
have put up too many thoughts together and chased
them where-ever{sic} they would double, Bertie; so
just write to me like a good fellow, and tell me that I
am an ass. Until I have that comforting assurance, I
shall place a quarantine upon everything which could
conceivably be offensive to you.

Does not lunacy strike you, Bertie, as being a very
eerie thing? It is a disease of the soul. To think that you

may have a man of noble mind, full of every lofty aspiration, and that a gross physical cause, such as the fall of a spicule of bone from the inner table of his skull on to the surface of the membrane which covers his brain, may have the ultimate effect of turning him into an obscene creature with every bestial attribute! That a man's individuality should swing round from pole to pole, and yet that one life should contain these two contradictory personalities - is it not a wondrous thing?

I ask myself, where is the man, the very, very inmost essence of the man? See how much you may subtract from him without touching it. It does not lie in the limbs which serve him as tools, nor in the apparatus by which he is to digest, nor in that by which he is to inhale oxygen. All these are mere accessories, the slaves of the lord within. Where, then, is he? He does not lie in the features which are to express his emotions, nor in the eyes and ears which can be dispensed with by the blind and deaf. Nor is he in the bony framework which is the rack over which nature hangs her veil of flesh. In none of these things lies the essence of the man. And now what is left? An arched whitish putty-like mass, some fifty odd ounces in weight, with a number of white filaments hanging down from it, looking not unlike the medusae which float in our summer seas. But these filaments only serve to conduct nerve force to muscles and to organs which serve secondary purposes. They may themselves therefore be disregarded. Nor can we stop here in our elimination. This central mass of nervous matter may be pared down on all sides before we seem to get at the very seat of the soul. Suicides have shot away the front lobes of the brain, and have lived to repent it. Surgeons have cut down upon it and have removed sections.

Much of it is merely for the purpose of furnishing the springs of motion, and much for the reception of impressions. All this may be put aside as we search for the physical seat of what we call the soul - the spiritual part of the man. And what is left then? A little blob of matter, a handful of nervous dough, a few ounces of tissue, but there - somewhere there - lurks that impalpable seed, to which the rest of our frame is but the pod. The old philosophers who put the soul in the pineal gland were not right, but after all they were uncommonly near the mark.

You'll find my physiology even worse than my theology, Bertie. I have a way of telling stories backwards to you, which is natural enough when you consider that I always sit down to write under the influence of the last impressions which have come upon me. All this talk about the soul and the brain arises simply from the fact that I have been spending the last few weeks with a lunatic. And how it came about I will tell you as clearly as I can.

You remember that in my last I explained to you how restive I had been getting at home, and how my idiotic mistake had annoyed my father and had made my position here very uncomfortable. Then I mentioned, I think, that I had received a letter from Christie & Howden, the lawyers. Well, I brushed up my Sunday at, and my mother stood on a chair and landed me twice on the ear with a clothes brush, under the impression that she was making the collar of my overcoat look more presentable. With which accolade out I sallied into the world, the dear soul standing on the steps, peering after me and waving me success.

Well, I was in considerable trepidation when I reached

Sir A. C. Doyle

the office, for I am a much more nervous person than any of my friends will ever credit me with being. However, I was shown in at once to Mr. James Christie, a wiry, sharp, thin-lipped kind of man, with an abrupt manner, and that sort of Scotch precision of speech which gives the impression of clearness of thought behind it.

"I understand from Professor Maxwell that you have been looking about for an opening, Mr. Munro," said he.

Maxwell had said that he would give me a hand if he could; but you remember that he had a reputation for giving such promises rather easily. I speak of a man as I find him, and to me he has been an excellent friend.

"I should be very happy to hear of any opening," said I.

"Of your medical qualifications there is no need to speak," he went on, running his eyes all over me in the most questioning way. "Your Bachelorship of Medicine will answer for that. But Professor Maxwell thought you peculiarly fitted for this vacancy for physical reasons. May I ask you what your weight is?"

"Fourteen stone."

"And you stand, I should judge, about six feet high?"

"Precisely."

"Accustomed too, as I gather, to muscular exercise of every kind. Well, there can be no question that you are the very man for the post, and I shall be very happy to recommend you to Lord Saltire."

"You forget," said I, "that I have not yet heard what the position is, or the terms which you offer."

He began to laugh at that. "It was a little precipitate on my part," said he; "but I do not think that we are likely to quarrel as to position or terms. You may have heard perhaps of the sad misfortune of our client, Lord Saltire? Not? To put it briefly then, his son, the Hon. James Derwent, the heir to the estates and the only child, was struck down by the sun while fishing without his hat last July. His mind has never recovered from the shock, and he has been ever since in a chronic state of moody sullenness which breaks out every now and then into violent mania. His father will not allow him to be removed from Lochtully Castle, and it is his desire that a medical man should stay there in constant attendance upon his son. Your physical strength would of course be very useful in restraining those violent attacks of which I have spoken. The remuneration will be twelve pounds a month, and you would be required to take over your duties to-morrow."

I walked home, my dear Bertie, with a bounding heart, and the pavement like cotton wool under my feet. I found just eightpence in my pocket, and I spent the whole of it on a really good cigar with which to celebrate the occasion. Old Cullingworth has always had a very high opinion of lunatics for beginners. "Get a lunatic, my boy! Get a lunatic!" he used to say. Then it was not only the situation, but the fine connection that it opened up. I seemed to see exactly what would happen. There would be illness in the family, - Lord Saltire himself perhaps, or his wife. There would be no time to send for advice. I would be consulted. I would gain their confidence and become their family attendant. They would recommend me to their wealthy friends. It was all as clear as possible. I was debating before I reached home whether it would be worth my while to give up a lucrative country practice in order to take the Professorship which might be offered me.

My father took the news philosophically enough, with some rather sardonic remark about my patient and me being well qualified to keep each other company. But to my mother it was a flash of joy, followed by a thunderclap of consternation. I had only three under-shirts, the best of my linen had gone to Belfast to be refronted and recuffed, the night-gowns were not marked yet - there were a dozen of those domestic difficulties of which the mere male never thinks. A dreadful vision of Lady Saltire looking over my things and finding the heel out of one of my socks obsessed my mother. Out we trudged together, and before evening her soul was at rest, and I had mortgaged in advance my first month's salary. She was great, as we walked home, upon the grand people into whose service I was to enter. "As a matter of fact, my dear," said she, "they are in a sense relations of yours. You are very closely allied to the Percies, and the Saltires have Percy blood in them also. They are only a cadet branch, and you are close upon the main line; but still it is not for us to deny the connection." She brought a cold sweat out upon me by suggesting that she should make things easy by writing to Lord Saltire and explaining our respective positions. Several times during the evening I heard her murmur complacently that they were only the cadet branch.

Am I not the slowest of story-tellers? But you encourage me to it by your sympathetic interest in details. However, I shall move along a little faster now. Next morning I was off to Lochtully, which, as you know, is in the north of Perthshire. It stands three miles from the station, a great gray pinnacled house, with two towers cocking out above the fir woods, like a hare's ears from a tussock of grass. As we drove up to the door I felt pretty solemn - not at all as the main line should do when it condescends to visit the cadet branch. Into the hall as I entered came a grave learned-looking man, with whom in my nervousness I was about to shake hands cordially. Fortunately he forestalled the impending embrace by explaining that he was the butler. He showed me into a small study, where everything stank of varnish and morocco leather, there to await the great man. He proved when he came to be a much less formidable figure than his retainer - indeed, I felt thoroughly at my ease with him from the moment he opened his mouth. He is grizzled, red-faced, sharp-featured, with a prying and yet benevolent expression, very human and just a trifle vulgar. His wife, however, to whom I was afterwards introduced, is a most depressing person, - pale, cold, hatchet-faced, with drooping eyelids and very prominent blue veins at her temples. She froze me up again just as I was budding out under the influence of her husband. However, the thing that interested me most of all was to see my patient, to whose room I was taken by Lord Saltire after we had had a cup of tea.

The room was a large bare one, at the end of a long corridor. Near the door was seated a footman, placed there to fill up the gap between two doctors, and looking considerably relieved at my advent. Over by the window (which was furnished with a wooden guard, like that of a nursery) sat a tall, yellow-haired, yellow-bearded, young man, who raised a pair of startled blue eyes as we entered. He was turning over the pages of a bound copy of the Illustrated London News.

"James," said Lord Saltire, "this is Dr. Stark Munro, who has come to look after you."

My patient mumbled something in his beard, which seemed to me suspiciously like "Damn Dr. Stark Munro!" The peer evidently thought the same, for he led me aside by the elbow.

"I don't know whether you have been told that James is a little rough in his ways at present," said he; "his whole nature has deteriorated very much since this calamity came upon him. You must not be offended by anything he may say or do."

"Not in the least," said I.

"There is a taint of this sort upon my wife's side," I whispered the little lord; "her uncle's symptoms were identical. Dr. Peterson says that the sunstroke was only the determining cause. The predisposition was already there. I may tell you that the footman will always be in the next room, so that you can call him if you need his assistance."

Well, it ended by lord and lacquey moving off, and leaving me with my patient. I thought that I should lose no time in establishing a kindly relation with him, so I drew a chair over to his sofa and began to ask him a few questions about his health and habits. Not a word could I get out of him in reply. He sat as sullen as a mule, with a kind of sneer about his handsome face, which showed me very well that he had heard everything. I tried this and tried that, but not a syllable could I get from him; so at last I turned from him and began to look over some illustrated papers on the table. He doesn't read, it seems, and will do nothing but look at pictures. Well, I was sitting like this with my back half turned, when you can imagine my surprise to feel something plucking gently at me, and to see a great brown hand trying to slip its way into my coat pocket. I caught at the wrist and turned swiftly round, but too late to prevent my handkerchief being whisked out and concealed behind the Hon. James Derwent, who sat grinning at me like a mischievous monkey.

"Come, I may want that," said I, trying to treat the matter as a joke.

He used some language which was more scriptural than religious. I saw that he did not mean giving it up, but I was determined not to let him get the upper hand over me. I grabbed for the handkerchief; and he, with a snarl, caught my hand in both of his. He had a powerful grip, but I managed to get his wrist and to give it a wrench round, until, with a howl, he dropped my property.

"What fun," said I, pretending to laugh. "Let us try again. Now, you take it up, and see if I can get it again."

But he had had enough of that game. Yet he appeared to be better humoured than before the incident, and I got a few short answers to the questions which I put to him.

And here comes in the text which started me preaching about lunacy at the beginning of this letter. WHAT a marvellous thing it is! This man, from all I

Sir A. C. Doyle

can learn of him, has suddenly swung clean over from one extreme of character to the other. Every plus has in an instant become a minus. He's another man, but in the same case. I am told that he used to be (only a few months ago, mind you) most fastidious in dress and speech. Now he is a foul-tongued rough! He had a nice taste in literature. Now he stares at you if you speak of Shakespeare. Queerest of all, he used to be a very high-and-dry Tory in his opinions. He is fond now of airing the most democratic views, and in a needlessly offensive way. When I did get on terms with him at last, I found that there was nothing on which he could be drawn on to talk so soon as on politics. In substance, I am bound to say that I think his new views are probably saner than his old ones, but the insanity lies in his sudden reasonless change and in his violent blurts of speech.

It was some weeks, however, before I gained his confidence, so far as to be able to hold a real conversation with him. For a long time he was very sullen and suspicious, resenting the constant watch which I kept upon him. This could not be relaxed, for he was full of the most apish tricks. One day he got hold of my tobacco pouch, and stuffed two ounces of my tobacco into the long barrel of an Eastern gun which hangs on the wall. He jammed it all down with the ramrod, and I was never able to get it up again. Another time he threw an earthenware spittoon through the window, and would have sent the clock after it had I not prevented him. Every day I took him for a two hours' constitutional, save when it rained, and then we walked religiously for the same space up and down the room. Heh! but it was a deadly, dreary, kind of life.

I was supposed to have my eye upon him all day, with

a two-hour interval every afternoon and an evening to myself upon Fridays. But then what was the use of an evening to myself when there was no town near, and I had no friends whom I could visit? I did a fair amount of reading, for Lord Saltire let me have the run of his library. Gibbon gave me a couple of enchanting weeks. You know the effect that he produces. You seem to be serenely floating upon a cloud, and looking down on all these pigmy armies and navies, with a wise Mentor ever at your side to whisper to you the inner meaning of all that majestic panorama.

Now and again young Derwent introduced some excitement into my dull life. On one occasion when we were walking in the grounds, he suddenly snatched up a spade from a grass-plot, and rushed at an inoffensive under-gardener. The man ran screaming for his life, with my patient cursing at his very heels, and me within a few paces of him. When I at last laid my hand on his collar, he threw down his weapon and burst into shrieks of laughter. It was only mischief and not ferocity; but when that under-gardener saw us coming after that he was off with a face like a cream cheese. At night the attendant slept in a camp-bed at the foot of the patient's, and my room was next door, so that I could be called if necessary. No, it was not a very exhilarating life!

We used to go down to family meals when there were no visitors; and there we made a curious quartette: Jimmy (as he wished me to call him) glum and silent; I with the tail of my eye always twisted round to him; Lady Saltire with her condescending eyelids and her blue veins; and the good-natured peer, fussy and genial, but always rather subdued in the presence of his wife. She looked as if a glass of good wine would do her good, and he as if he would be the better for abstinence; and so, in accordance with the usual lopsidedness of life, he drank freely, and she took nothing but lime-juice and water. You cannot imagine a more ignorant, intolerant, narrow-minded woman than she. If she had only been content to be silent and hidden that small brain of hers, it would not have mattered; but there was no end to her bitter and exasperating clacking. What was she after all but a thin pipe for conveying disease from one generation to another? She was bounded by insanity upon the north and upon the south. I resolutely set myself to avoid all argument with her; but she knew, with her woman's instinct, that we were as far apart as the poles, and took a pleasure in waving the red flag before me. One day she was waxing eloquent as to the crime of a minister of an Episcopal church performing any service in a Presbyterian chapel. Some neighbouring minister had done it, it seems; and if he had been marked down in a pot house she could not have spoken with greater loathing. I suppose that my eyes were less under control than my tongue, for she suddenly turned upon me with:

"I see that you don't agree with me, Dr. Munro."

I replied quietly that I did not, and tried to change the conversation; but she was not to be shaken off.

"Why not, may I ask?"

I explained that in my opinion the tendency of the age was to break down those ridiculous doctrinal points which are so useless, and which have for so long set people by the ears. I added that I hoped the time was soon coming when good men of all creeds would throw this lumber overboard and join hands together.

She half rose, almost speechless with indignation.

"I presume," said she, "that you are one of those people who would separate the Church from the State?"

"Most certainly," I answered.

She stood erect in a kind of cold fury, and swept out of the room. Jimmy began to chuckle, and his father looked perplexed.

"I am sorry that my opinions are offensive to Lady Saltire," I remarked.

"Yes, yes; it's a pity; a pity," said he "well, well, we must say what we think; but it's a pity you think it - a very great pity."

I quite expected to get my dismissal over this business, and indeed, indirectly I may say that I did so. From that day Lady Saltire was as rude to me as she could be, and never lost an opportunity of making attacks upon what she imagined to be my opinions. Of these I never took the slightest notice; but at last on an evil day she went for me point-blank, so that there was no getting away from her. It was just at the end of lunch, when the footman had left the room. She had been talking about Lord Saltire's going up to London to vote upon some question in the House of Lords.

"Perhaps, Dr. Munro," said she, turning acidly upon me, "that is also an institution which has not been fortunate enough to win your approval."

"It is a question, Lady Saltire, which I should much prefer not to discuss," I answered.

"Oh, you might just as well have the courage of your convictions," said she. "Since you desire to despoil the National Church, it is natural enough that you should wish also to break up the Constitution. I have heard that an atheist is always a red republican."

Lord Saltire rose, wishing, I have no doubt, to put an end to the conversation. Jimmy and I rose also; and suddenly I saw that instead of moving towards the door he was going to his mother. Knowing his little tricks, I passed my hand under his arm, and tried to steer him away. She noticed it, however, and interfered.

"Did you wish to speak to me, James?"

"I want to whisper in your ear, mother."

"Pray don't excite yourself, sir," said I, again attempting to detain him. Lady Saltire arched her aristocratic eyebrows.

"I think, Dr. Munro, that you push your authority rather far when you venture to interfere between a mother and her son," said she. What was it, my poor dear boy?"

Jimmy bent down and whispered something in her ear. The blood rushed into her pale face, and she sprang from him as if he had struck her. Jimmy began to snigger.

"This is your doing, Dr. Munro," she cried furiously. "You have corrupted my son's mind, and encouraged him to insult his mother."

"My dear! My dear!" said her husband soothingly, and I quietly led the recalcitrant Jimmy up stairs. I asked him what it was that he had said to his mother, but got only chuckles in reply.

I had a presentiment that I should hear more of the matter; and I was not wrong. Lord Saltire called me into his study in the evening.

"The fact is, doctor," said he, "that Lady Saltire has been extremely annoyed and grieved about what occurred at lunch to-day. Of course, you can imagine that such an expression coming from her own son, shocked her more than I can tell."

"I assure you, Lord Saltire," said I, "that I have no idea at all what passed between Lady Saltire and my patient."

"Well," said he, "without going into details, I may say that what he whispered was a blasphemous wish, most coarsely expressed, as to the future of that Upper House to which I have the honor to belong."

"I am very sorry," said I, "and I assure you that I have never encouraged him in his extreme political views, which seem to me to be symptoms of his disease."

"I am quite convinced that what you say is true," he answered; "but Lady Saltire is unhappily of the opinion that you have instilled these ideas into him. You know that it is a little difficult sometimes to reason with a lady. However, I have no doubt that all may be smoothed over if you would see Lady Saltire and assure her that she has misunderstood your views upon this point, and that you are personally a supporter of a Hereditary Chamber."

It put me in a tight corner, Bertie; but my mind was instantly made up. From the first word I had read my dismissal in every uneasy glance of his little eyes.

"I am afraid," said I, "that that is rather further than I am prepared to go. I think that since there has been for some weeks a certain friction between Lady Saltire and myself, it would perhaps be as well that I should resign the post which I hold in your household. I shall be happy, however, to remain here until you have found some one to take over my duties."

"Well, I am sorry it has come to this, and yet it may be that you are right," said he, with an expression of relief; "as to James, there need be no difficulty about that, for Dr. Patterson could come in tomorrow morning."

"Then to-morrow morning let it be," I answered.

"Very good, Dr. Munro; I will see that you have your cheque before you go."

So there was the end of all my fine dreams about aristocratic practices and wonderful introductions! I believe the only person in the whole house who regretted me was Jimmy, who was quite downcast at the news. His grief, however, did not prevent him from brushing my new top-hat the wrong way on the morning that I left. I did not notice it until I reached the station, and a most undignified object I must have looked when I took my departure.

So ends the history of a failure. I am, as you know, inclined to fatalism, and do not believe that such a thing as chance exists; so I am bound to think that this experience was given to me for some end. It was a preliminary canter for the big race, perhaps. My mother was disappointed, but tried to show it as little as possible. My father was a little sardonic over the matter. I fear that the gap between us widens. By the way, an extraordinary card arrived from Cullingworth during my absence. "You are my man," said he; "mind that I am to have you when I want you." There was no date and no address, but the postmark was Bradfield in the north of England. Does it mean nothing? Or may it mean everything? We must wait and see.

Good-bye, old man. Let me hear equally fully about your own affairs. How did the Rattray business go off?

V.

MERTON ON THE MOORS,
5th March, 1882.

I was so delighted, my dear chap, to have your
assurance that nothing that I have said or could say
upon the subject of religion could offend you. It is
difficult to tell you how pleased and relieved I was at
your cordial letter. I have no one to whom I can talk
upon such matters. I am all driven inwards, and
thought turns sour when one lets it stagnate like that. It
is a grand thing to be able to tell it all to a sympathetic
listener - and the more so perhaps when he looks at it
all from another standpoint. It steadies and sobers one.

Those whom I love best are those who have least
sympathy with my struggles. They talk about having
faith, as if it could be done by an act of volition. They
might as well tell me to have black hair instead of red.
I might simulate it perhaps by refusing to use my
reason at all in religious matters. But I will never be
traitor to the highest thing that God has given me. I
WILL use it. It is more moral to use it and go wrong,
than to forego it and be right. It is only a little foot-
rule, and I have to measure Mount Everest with it; but
it's all I have, and I'll never give it up while there's
breath between my lips.

With all respect to you, Bertie, it is very easy to be

orthodox. A man who wanted mental peace and material advancement in this world would certainly choose to be so. As Smiles says - "A dead fish can float with the stream, but it takes a man to swim against it." What could be more noble than the start and the starter of Christianity? How beautiful the upward struggle of an idea, like some sweet flower blossoming out amon-gst rubble and cinders! But, alas! to say that this idea was a final idea! That this scheme of thought was above the reason! That this gentle philosopher was that supreme intelligence to which we cannot even imagine a personality without irreverence! - all this will come to rank with the strangest delusions of mankind. And then how clouded has become that fine daybreak of Christianity! Its representatives have risen from the manger to the palace, from the fishing smack to the House of Lords. Nor is that other old potentate in the Vatican, with his art treasures, his guards, and his cellars of wine in a more logical position. They are all good and talented men, and in the market of brains are worth perhaps as much as they get. But how can they bring themselves to pose as the representatives of a creed, which, as they themselves expound it, is based upon humility, poverty, and self-denial? Not one of them who would not quote with approval the parable of the Wedding Guest. But try putting one of them out of their due precedence at the next Court reception. It happened some little time ago with a Cardinal, and England rang with his protests. How blind not to see how they would spring at one leap into the real first place if they would but resolutely claim the last as the special badge of their master!

What can we know? What are we all? Poor silly half-brained things peering out at the infinite, with the aspirations of angels and the instincts of beasts. But surely all will be well with us. If not, then He who made us is evil, which is not to be thought. Surely, then, all must go very well with us!

I feel ashamed when I read this over. My mind fills in all the trains of thought of which you have the rude ends peeping out from this tangle. Make what you can of it, dear Bertie, and believe that it all comes from my innermost heart. Above all may I be kept from becoming a partisan, and tempering with truth in order to sustain a case. Let me but get a hand on her skirt, and she may drag me where she will, if she will but turn her face from time to time that I may know her.

You'll see from the address of this letter, Bertie, that I have left Scotland and am in Yorkshire. I have been here three months, and am now on the eve of leaving under the strangest circumstances and with the queerest prospects. Good old Cullingworth has turned out a trump, as I always knew he would. But, as usual, I am beginning at the wrong end, so here goes to give you an idea of what has been happening.

I told you in my last about my lunacy adventure and my ignominious return from Lochtully Castle. When I had settled for the flannel vests which my mother had ordered so lavishly I had only five pounds left out of my pay. With this, as it was the first money that I had ever earned im{sic} my life, I bought her a gold bangle, so behold me reduced at once to my usual empty pocketed condition. Well, it was something just to feel that I HAD earned money. It gave me an assurance that I might again.

I had not been at home more than a few days when my

father called me into the study after breakfast one morning and spoke very seriously as to our financial position. He began the interview by unbuttoning his waistcoat and asking me to listen at his fifth intercostal space, two inches from the left sternal line. I did so, and was shocked to hear a well-marked mitral regurgitant murmur.

"It is of old standing," said he, "but of late I have had a puffiness about the ankles and some renal symptoms which show me that it is beginning to tell."

I tried to express my grief and sympathy, but he cut me short with some asperity.

"The point is," said he, "that no insurance office would accept my life, and that I have been unable, owing to competition and increased expenses, to lay anything by. If I die soon (which, between ourselves, is by no means improbable), I must leave to your care your mother and the children. My practice is so entirely a personal one that I cannot hope to be able to hand over to you enough to afford a living."

I thought of Cullingworth's advice about going where you are least known. "I think," said I, "that, my chances would be better away from here."

"Then you must lose no time in establishing yourself," said he. "Your position would be one of great responsibility if anything were to happen to me just now. I had hoped that you had found an excellent opening with the Saltires; but I fear that you can hardly expect to get on in the world, my boy, if you insult your employer's religious and political view at his own table."

It wasn't a time to argue, so I said nothing. My father took a copy of the Lancet out of his desk, and turned up an advertisement which he had marked with a blue pencil. "Read this!" said he.

I've got it before me as I write. It runs thus: Qualified Assistant. Wanted at once in a large country and colliery practice. Thorough knowledge of obstetrics and dispensing indispensable. Ride and drive. L70 a year. Apply Dr, Horton Merton on the Moors, Yorkshire."

"There might be an opening there," said he. "I know Horton, and I am convinced that I can get you the appointment. It would at least give you the opportunity of looking round and seeing whether there was any vacancy there. How do you think it would suit you?"

Of course I could only answer that I was willing to turn my hand to anything. But that interview has left a mark upon me - a heavy ever-present gloom away at the back of my soul, which I am conscious of even when the cause of it has for a moment gone out of my thoughts.

I had enough to make a man serious before, when I had to face the world without money or interest. But now to think of the mother and my sisters and little Paul all leaning upon me when I cannot stand myself - it is a nightmare. Could there be anything more dreadful in life than to have those whom you love looking to you for help and to be unable to give it? But perhaps it won't come to that. Perhaps my father may hold his own for years. Come what may, I am bound to think that all things are ordered for the best; though when the good is a furlong off, and we with our beetle eyes can only see three inches, it takes some confidence in general principles to pull us through.

Well, it was all fixed up; and down I came to Yorkshire. I wasn't in the best of spirits when I started, Bertie, but they went down and down as I neared my destination. How people can dwell in such places passes my comprehension. What can life offer them to make up for these mutilations of the face of Nature? No woods, little grass, spouting chimneys, slate-coloured streams, sloping mounds of coke and slag, topped by the great wheels and pumps of the mines. Cinder-strewn paths, black as though stained by the weary miners who toil along them, lead through the tarnished fields to the rows of smoke-stained cottages. How can any young unmarried man accept such a lot while there's an empty hammock in the navy, or a berth in a merchant forecastle? How many shillings a week is the breath of the ocean worth? It seems to me that if I were a poor man - well, upon my word, that "if" is rather funny when I think that many of the dwellers in those smoky cottages have twice my salary with half my expenses.

Well, as I said, my spirits sank lower and lower until they got down into the bulb, when on looking through the gathering gloom I saw "Merton" printed on the lamps of a dreary dismal station. I got out, and was standing beside my trunk and my hat-box, waiting for a porter, when up came a cheery-looking fellow and asked me whether I was Dr. Stark Munro. "I'm Horton," said he; and shook hands cordially.

In that melancholy place the sight of him was like a fire on a frosty night. He was gaily dressed in the first place, check trousers, white waistcoat, a flower in his button hole. But the look of the man was very much to my heart. He was ruddy checked and black eyed, with a jolly stout figure and an honest genial smile. I felt as we clinched hands in the foggy grimy station that I had met a man and a friend.

His carriage was waiting, and we drove out to his residence, The Myrtles, where I was speedily introduced both to his family and his practice. The former is small, and the latter enormous. The wife is dead; but her mother, Mrs. White, keeps house for him; and there are two dear little girls, about five and seven. Then there is an unqualified assistant, a young Irish student, who, with the three maids, the coachman, and the stable boy, make up the whole establishment. When I tell you that we give four horses quite as much as they can do, you will have an idea of the ground we cover.

The house, a large square brick one, standing in its own grounds, is built on a small hill in an oasis of green fields. Beyond this, however, on every side the veil of smoke hangs over the country, with the mine pumps and the chimneys bristling out of it. It would be a dreadful place for an idle man: but we are all so busy that we have hardly time to think whether there's a view or not.

Day and night we are at work; and yet the three months have been very pleasant ones to look back upon.

I'll give you an idea of what a day's work is like. We breakfast about nine o'clock, and immediately afterwards the morning patients begin to drop in. Many of them are very poor people, belonging to the colliery clubs, the principle of which is, that the members pay a little over a halfpenny a week all the year round, well or ill, in return for which they get medicine and attendance free. "Not much of a catch for the doctors," you would say, but it is astonishing what competition there is among them to get the appointment. You see it is a certainty for one thing, and it leads indirectly to other little extras. Besides, it amounts up surprisingly. I have no doubt that Horton has five or six hundred a year from his clubs alone. On the other hand, you can imagine that club patients, since they pay the same in any case, don't let their ailments go very far before they are round in the consulting room.

Well, then, by half-past nine we are in full blast. Horton is seeing the better patients in the consulting room, I am interviewing the poorer ones in the waiting room, and McCarthy, the Irishman, making up prescriptions as hard as he can tear. By the club rules, patients are bound to find their own bottles and corks.

They generally remember the bottle, but always forget the cork. "Ye must pay a pinny or ilse put your forefinger in," says McCarthy. They have an idea that all the strength of the medicine goes if the bottle is open, so they trot off with their fingers stuck in the necks. They have the most singular notions about medicines. "It's that strong that a spoon will stand oop in't!" is one man's description. Above all, they love to have two bottles, one with a solution of citric acid, and the other with carbonate of soda. When the mixture begins to fizz, they realise that there is indeed a science of medicine.

This sort of work, with vaccinations, bandagings, and minor surgery, takes us to nearly eleven o'clock, when we assemble in Horton's room to make out the list. All the names of patients under treatment are pinned upon a big board. We sit round with note books open, and distribute those who must be seen between us. By the time this is done and the horses in, it is half-past eleven. Then away we all FLY upon our several tasks: Horton in a carriage and pair to see the employers; I in a dog cart to see the employed; and McCarthy on his good Irish legs to see those chronic cases to which a qualified man can do no good, and an unqualified no harm.

Well, we all work back again by two o'clock, when we find dinner waiting for us. We may or may not have finished our rounds. If not away we go again. If we have, Horton dictates his prescriptions, and strides off to bed with his black clay pipe in his mouth. He is the most abandoned smoker I have ever met with, collecting the dottles of his pipes in the evening, and smoking them the next morning before breakfast in the stable yard. When he has departed for his nap, McCarthy and I get to work on the medicine. There are, perhaps, fifty bottles to put up, with pills, ointment, etc. It is quite half-past four before we have them all laid out on the shelf addressed to the respective invalids. Then we have an hour or so of quiet, when we smoke or read, or box with the coachman in the harness room. After tea the evening's work commences. From six to nine people are coming in for their medicine, or fresh patients wishing advice. When these are settled we have to see again any very grave cases which may be on the list; and so, about ten o'clock, we may hope to have another smoke, and perhaps a game of cards. Then it is a rare thing for a night to pass without one or other of us having to trudge off to a case which may take us two hours, or may take us ten. Hard work, as you see; but Horton is such a good chap, and works so hard himself, that one does not mind what one does. And then we are all like brothers in the house; our talk is just a rattle of chaff, and the patients are as homely as ourselves, so that the work becomes quite a pleasure to all of us.

Yes, Horton is a real right-down good fellow. His heart is broad and kind and generous. There is nothing petty in the man. He loves to see those around him happy; and the sight of his sturdy figure and jolly red face goes far to make them so. Nature meant him to be a healer; for he brightens up a sick room as he did the Merton station when first I set eyes upon him. Don't imagine from my description that he is in any way soft, however. There is no one on whom one could be less likely to impose. He has a temper which is easily aflame and as easily appeased. A mistake in the dispensing may wake it up and then he bursts into the surgery like a whiff of cast wind, his checks red, his whiskers bristling, and his eyes malignant. The day-book is banged, the bottles rattled, the counter thumped, and then he is off again with five doors slamming behind him. We can trace his progress when the black mood is on him by those dwindling slams. Perhaps it is that McCarthy has labelled the cough mixture as the eye-wash, or sent an empty pillbox with an exhortation to take one every four hours. In any case the cyclone comes and goes, and by the next meal all is peace once more.

I said that the patients were very homely. Any one who is over-starched might well come here to be unstiffened. I confess that I did not quite fall in with it at once. When on one of my first mornings a club patient with his bottle under his arm came up to me and asked me if I were the doctor's man, I sent him on to see the groom in the stable. But soon one falls into the humour of it. There is no offence meant; and why should any be taken? They are kindly, generous folk; and if they pay no respect to your profession in the abstract, and so rather hurt your dignity, they will be as leal and true as possible to yourself if you can win their respect. I like the grip of their greasy and blackened hands.

Another peculiarity of the district is that many of the manufacturers and colliery owners have risen from the workmen, and have (in some cases at least) retained their old manners and even their old dress. The other day Mrs. White, Horton's mother-in-law, had a violent sick headache, and, as we are all very fond of the kind old lady, we were trying to keep things as quiet as possible down-stairs. Suddenly there came a bang! bang! bang! at the knocker; and then in an instant another rattling series of knocks, as if a tethered donkey were trying to kick in the panel. After all our efforts for silence it was exasperating. I rushed to the door to find a seedy looking person just raising his hand to commence a fresh bombardment. "What on earth's the matter?" I asked, only I may have been a little more emphatic. "Pain in the jaw," said he. "You needn't make such a noise," said I; "other people are ill besides you." "If I pay my money, young man, I'll make such noise as I like." And actually in cold blood he commenced a fresh assault upon the door. He would have gone on with his devil's tattoo all morning if I had not led him down the path and seen him off the premises. An hour afterwards Horton whirled into the surgery, with a trail of banged doors behind him. "What's this about Mr. Usher, Munro?" he asked. "He says that you were violent towards him." "There was a club patient here who kept on banging the knocker," said I; "I was afraid that he would disturb Mrs. White, and so I made him stop." Horton's eyes began to twinkle. "My boy," said he, "that club patient, as you call him, is the richest man in Merton, and worth a hundred a year to me." I have no doubt that he appeased him by some tale of my disgrace and degradation; but I have not heard anything of the matter since.

It has been good for me to be here, Bertie. It has brought me in close contact with the working classes, and made me realise what fine people they are. Because one drunkard goes home howling on a Saturday night, we are too apt to overlook the ninety-nine decent folk by their own firesides. I shall not make that mistake any more. The kindliness of the poor to the poor makes a man sick of himself. And their sweet patience! Depend upon it, if ever there is a popular rising, the wrongs which lead to it must be monstrous and indefensible. I think the excesses of the French Revolution are dreadful enough in themselves, but much more so as an index to the slow centuries of misery against which they were a mad protest. And then the wisdom of the poor! It is amusing to read the glib newspaper man writing about the ignorance of the masses. They don't know the date of Magna Charta, or whom John of Gaunt married; but put a practical up-to-date problem before them, and see how unerringly they take the right side. Didn't they put the Reform Bill through in the teeth of the opposition of the majority of the so-called educated classes? Didn't they back the North against the South when nearly all our leaders went wrong? When universal arbitration and the suppression of the liquor traffic comes, is it not sure to be from the pressure of these humble folks? They look at life with clearer and more unselfish eyes. It's an axiom, I think, that to heighten a nation's wisdom you must lower its franchise.

I often have my doubts, Bertie, if there is such a thing as the existence of evil? If we could honestly convince ourselves that there was not, it would help us so much in formulating a rational religion. But don't let us strain truth even for such an object as that. I must confess that there are some forms of vice, cruelty for example, for which it is hard to find any explanation, save indeed that it is a degenerate survival of that war-like ferocity which may once have been of service in helping to protect the community. No; let me be frank, and say that I can't make cruelty fit into my scheme. But when you find that other evils, which seem at first sight black enough, really tend in the long run to the good of mankind, it may be hoped that those which continue to puzzle us may at last be found to serve the same end in some fashion which is now inexplicable.

It seems to me that the study of life by the physician vindicates the moral principles of right and wrong. But when you look closely it is a question whether that which is a wrong to the present community may not prove to have been a right to the interests of posterity. That sounds a little foggy; but I will make my meaning more clear when I say that I think right and wrong are both tools which are being wielded by those great hands which are shaping the destinies of the universe, that both are making for improvement; but that the action of the one is immediate, and that of the other more slow, but none the less certain. Our own distinction of right and wrong is founded too much upon the immediate convenience of the community, and does not inquire sufficiently deeply into the ultimate effect.

I have my own views about Nature's methods, though I feel that it is rather like a beetle giving his opinions upon the milky way. However, they have the merit of being consoling; for if we could conscientiously see that sin served a purpose, and a good one, it would take some of the blackness out of life. It seems to me, then, that Nature, still working on the lines of evolution, strengthens the race in two ways. The one is by improving those who are morally strong, which is done by increased knowledge and broadening religious views; the other, and hardly less important, is by the killing off and extinction of those who are morally weak. This is accomplished by drink and immorality. These are really two of the most important forces which work for the ultimate perfection of the race. I picture them as two great invisible hands hovering over the garden of life and plucking up the weeds. Looked at in one's own day, one can only see that they produce degradation and misery. But at the end of a third generation from then, what has happened? The line of the drunkard and of the debauchee, physically as well as morally weakened, is either extinct or on the way towards it. Struma, tubercle, nervous disease, have all lent a hand towards the pruning off of that rotten branch, and the average of the race is thereby improved. I believe from the little that I have seen of life, that it is a law which acts with startling swiftness, that a majority of drunkards never perpetuate their species at all, and that when the curse is hereditary, the second generation generally sees the end of it.

Don't misunderstand me, and quote me as saying that it is a good thing for a nation that it should have many drunkards. Nothing of the kind. What I say is, that if a nation has many morally weak people, then it is good that there should be a means for checking those weaker strains. Nature has her devices, and drink is among them. When there are no more drunkards and reprobates, it means that the race is so advanced that it no longer needs such rough treatment. Then the all-wise Engineer will speed us along in some other fashion.

I've been thinking a good deal lately about this question of the uses of evil, and of how powerful a tool it is in the hands of the Creator. Last night the whole thing crystallised out quite suddenly into a small set of verses. Please jump them if they bore you.

WITH EITHER HAND.

1.

> God's own best will bide the test,
> And God's own worst will fall;
> But, best or worst or last or first,
> He ordereth it all.

2.

> For ALL is good, if understood,
> (Ah, could we understand!)
> And right and ill are tools of skill
> Held in His either hand.

3.

> The harlot and the anchorite,
> The martyr and the rake,
> Deftly He fashions each aright,
> Its vital part to take.

4.

Wisdom He makes to guide the sap
Where the high blossoms be;
And Lust to kill the weaker branch,
And Drink to trim the tree.

5.

And Holiness that so the bole
Be solid at the core;
And Plague and Fever, that the whole
Be changing evermore.

6.

He strews the microbes in the lung,
The blood-clot in the brain;
With test and test He picks the best,
Then tests them once again.

7.

He tests the body and the mind,
He rings them o'er and o'er;
And if they crack, He throws them back,
And fashions them once more.

8.

He chokes the infant throat with slime,
He sets the ferment free;
He builds the tiny tube of lime
That blocks the artery.

Sir A. C. Doyle

9.

> He lets the youthful dreamer store
> Great projects in his brain,
> Until he drops the fungus spore
> That smears them out again.

10.

> He stores the milk that feeds the babe,
> He dulls the tortured nerve;
> He gives a hundred joys of sense
> Where few or none might serve.

11.

> And still he trains the branch of good
> Where the high blossoms be,
> And wieldeth still the shears of ill
> To prune and prune His tree.

12.

> So read I this - and as I try
> To write it clear again,
> I feel a second finger lie
> Above mine on the pen.

13.

> Dim are these peering eyes of mine,
> And dark what I have seen.
> But be I wrong, the wrong is Thine,
> Else had it never been.

I am quite ashamed of having been so didactic. But it is fine to think that sin may have an object and work towards good. My father says that I seem to look upon the universe as if it were my property, and can't be happy until I know that all is right with it. Well, it does send a glow through me when I seem to catch a glimpse of the light behind the clouds.

And now for my big bit of news which is going to change my whole life. Whom do you think I had a letter from last Tuesday week? From Cullingworth, no less. It had no beginning, no end, was addressed all wrong, and written with a very thick quill pen upon the back of a prescription. How it ever reached me is a wonder. This is what he had to say: -

"Started here in Bradfield last June. Colossal success. My example must revolutionise medical practice. Rapidly making fortune. Have invention which is worth millions. Unless our Admiralty take it up shall make Brazil the leading naval power. Come down by next train on receiving this. Have plenty for you to do."

That was the whole of this extraordinary letter; it had no name to it, which was certainly reasonable enough, since no one else could have written it. Knowing Cullingworth as well as I did, I took it with reservations and deductions. How could he have made so rapid and complete a success in a town in which he must have been a complete stranger? It was incredible. And yet there must be some truth in it, or he would not invite me to come down and test it. On the whole, I thought that I had better move very cautiously in the matter; for I was happy and snug where I was, and kept on putting a little by, which I hoped would form a nucleus to start me in practice. It is only a few pounds up to date, but in a year or so it might mount to something. I wrote to Cullingworth, therefore, thanking him for having remembered me, and explaining how matters stood.

I had had great difficulty in finding an opening, I said, and now that I had one I was loth to give it up save for a permanency.

Ten days passed, during which Cullingworth was silent. Then came a huge telegram.

"Your letter to hand. Why not call me a liar at once? I tell you that I have seen thirty thousand patients in the last year. My actual takings have been over four thousand pounds. All patients come to me. Would not cross the street to see Queen Victoria. You can have all visiting, all surgery, all midwifery. Make what you like of it. Will guarantee three hundred pounds the first year."

Well, this began to look more like business - especially that last sentence. I took it to Horton, and asked his advice. His opinion was that I had nothing to lose and everything to gain. So it ended by my wiring back accepting the partnership - if it is a partnership - and to-morrow morning I am off to Bradfield with great hopes and a small portmanteau. I know how interested you are in the personality of Cullingworth - as every one is who comes, even at second hand, within range of his influence; and so you may rely upon it that I shall give you a very full and particular account of all that passes between us. I am looking forward immensely to seeing him again, and I trust we won't have any rows.

Goodbye, old chap. My foot is upon the threshold of fortune. Congratulate me.

Sir A. C. Doyle

VI.

1 THE PARADE, BRADFIELD,
7th March, 1882.

It is only two days since I wrote to you, my dear old chap, and yet I find myself loaded to the muzzle and at full cock again. I have come to Bradfield. I have seen old Cullingworth once more, and I have found that all he has told me is true. Yes; incredible as it sounded, this wonderful fellow seems to have actually built up a great practice in little more than a year. He really is, with all his eccentricities, a very remarkable man, Bertie. He doesn't seem to have a chance of showing his true powers in this matured civilisation. The law and custom hamper him. He is the sort of fellow who would come right to the front in a French Revolution. Or if you put him as Emperor over some of these little South American States, I believe that in ten years he would either be in his grave, or would have the Continent. Yes; Cullingworth is fit to fight for a higher stake than a medical practice, and on a bigger stage than an English provincial town. When I read of Aaron Burr in your history I always picture him as a man like C.

I had the kindest of leave takings from Horton. If he had been my brother he could not have been more affectionate. I could not have thought that I should grow so fond of a man in so short a time. He takes the keenest interest in my venture, and I am to write him a full account. He gave me as we parted a black old meerschaum which he had coloured himself - the last possible pledge of affection from a smoker. It was pleasant for me to feel that if all went wrong at Bradfield, I had a little harbour at Merton for which I could make. Still, of course, pleasant and instructive as the life there was, I could not shut my eyes to the fact that it would take a terribly long time before I could save enough to buy a share in a practice - a longer time probably than my poor father's strength would last. That telegram of Cullingworth's in which, as you may remember, he guaranteed me three hundred pounds in the first year, gave me hopes of a much more rapid career. You will agree with me, I am sure, that I did wisely to go to him.

I had an adventure upon the way to Bradfield. The carriage in which I was travelling contained a party of three, at whom I took the most casual of glances before settling down to the daily paper. There was an elderly lady, with a bright rosy face, gold spectacles, and a dash of red velvet in her bonnet. With her were two younger people, who I took to be her son and her daughter - the one a quiet, gentle-looking girl of twenty or so, dressed in black, and the other a short, thick-set young fellow, a year or two older. The two ladies sat by each other in the far corner, and the son (as I presume him to be) sat opposite me. We may have travelled an hour or more without my paying any attention to this little family party, save that I could not help hearing some talk between the two ladies. The younger, who was addressed as Winnie, had, as I noticed, a very sweet and soothing voice. She called the elder "mother," which showed that I was right as to the relationship.

I was sitting, then, still reading my paper, when I was surprised to get a kick on the shins from the young fellow opposite. I moved my legs, thinking that it was an accident, but an instant afterwards I received another and a harder one. I dropped my paper with a growl, but the moment that I glanced at him I saw how the matter stood. His foot was jerking spasmodically, his two hands clenched, and drumming against his breast, while his eyes were rolling upwards until only the rim of his iris was to be seen. I sprang upon him, tore open his collar, unbuttoned his waistcoat, and pulled his head down upon the seat. Crash went one of his heels through the carriage window, but I contrived to sit upon his knees while I kept hold of his two wrists.

"Don't be alarmed!" I cried it's epilepsy, and will soon pass!"

Glancing up, I saw that the little girl was sitting very pale and quiet in the corner. The mother had pulled a bottle out of her bag and was quite cool and helpful.

"He often has them," said she this is bromide."

"He is coming out," I answered; "you look after Winnie."

I blurted it out because her head seemed to rock as if she were going off; but the absurdity of the thing struck us all next moment, and the mother burst into a laugh in which the daughter and I joined. The son had opened his eyes and had ceased to struggle.

"I must really beg your pardon," said I, as I helped him up again. "I had not the advantage of knowing your other name, and I was in such a hurry that I had no time to think what I was saying."

They laughed again in the most good-humoured way, and, as soon as the young fellow had recovered, we all joined in quite a confidential conversation. It is wonderful how the intrusion of any of the realities of life brushes away the cobwebs of etiquette. In half an hour we knew all about each other, or at any rate I knew all about them. Mrs. La Force was the mother's name, a widow with these two children. They had given up housekeeping, and found it more pleasant to live in apartments, travelling from one watering place to another. Their one trouble was the nervous weakness of the son Fred. They were now on their way to Birchespool, where they hoped that he might get some good from the bracing air. I was able to recommend vegetarianism, which I have found to act like a charm in such cases. We had quite a spirited conversation, and I think that we were sorry on both sides when we came to the junction where they had to change. Mrs. La Force gave me her card, and I promised to call if ever I should be in Birchespool.

However, all this must be stupid enough to you. You know my little ways by this time, and you don't expect me to keep on the main line of my story. However, I am back on the rails now, and I shall try to remain there.

Well, it was nearly six o'clock, and evening was just creeping in when we drew up in Bradfield Station. The first thing I saw when I looked out of the window was Cullingworth, exactly the same as ever, striding in his jerky way down the platform, his coat flying open, his chin thrust forward (he is the most under-hung man I

Sir A. C. Doyle

have ever seen), and his great teeth all gleaming, like a good-natured blood-hound. He roared with delight when he saw me, wrung my hand, and slapped me enthusiastically upon the shoulder.

"My dear chap!" said he. "We'll clear this town out. I tell you, Munro, we won't leave a doctor in it. It's all they can do now to get butter to their bread; and when we get to work together they'll have to eat it dry. Listen to me, my boy! There are a hundred and twenty thousand folk in this town, all shrieking for advice, and there isn't a doctor who knows a rhubarb pill from a calculus. Man, we only have to gather them in. I stand and take the money until my arm aches."

"But how is it?" I asked, as we pushed our way through the crowd. Are there so few other doctors?"

"Few!" he roared. "By Crums, the streets are blocked with them. You couldn't fall out of a window in this town without killing a doctor. But of all the - - well, there, you'll see them for yourself. You walked to my house at Avonmouth, Munro. I don't let my friends walk to my house at Bradfield - eh, what?"

A well-appointed carriage with two fine black horses was drawn up at the station entrance. The smart coachman touched his hat as Cullingworth opened the door.

"Which of the houses, sir?" he asked.

Cullingworth's eyes shot round to me to see what I thought of such a query. Between ourselves I have not the slightest doubt that he had instructed the man to ask it. He always had a fine eye for effect, but he usually erred by underrating the intelligence of those around him.

"Ah!" said he, rubbing his chin like a man in doubt. "Well, I daresay dinner will be nearly ready. Drive to the town residential."

"Good gracious, Cullingworth!" said I as we started. "How many houses do you inhabit? It sounds as if you had bought the town."

"Well, well," said he, laughing, "we are driving to the house where I usually live. It suits us very well, though I have not been able to get all the rooms furnished yet. Then I have a little farm of a few hundred acres just outside the city. It is a pleasant place for the week ends, and we send the nurse and the child - - "

"My dear chap, I did not know that you had started a family!"

"Yes, it's an infernal nuisance; but still the fact remains. We get our butter and things from the farm. Then, of course, I have my house of business in the heart of the city."

"Consulting and waiting room, I suppose?"

He looked at me with a sort of half vexed, half amused expression. "You cannot rise to a situation, Munro," said he. "I never met a fellow with such a stodgy imagination. I'd trust you to describe a thing when you have seen it, but never to build up an idea of it beforehand."

"What's the trouble now?" I asked.

"Well, I have written to you about my practice, and I've wired to you about it, and here you sit asking me if I work it in two rooms. I'll have to hire the market square before I've finished, and then I won't have space to wag my elbows. Can your imagination rise to a great house with people waiting in every room, jammed in as tight as they'll fit, and two layers of them squatting in the cellar? Well, that's my house of business on an average day. The folk come in from the county fifty miles off, and eat bread and treacle on the doorstep, so as to be first in when the housekeeper comes down. The medical officer of health made an official complaint of the over-crowding of my waiting-rooms. They wait in the stables, and sit along the racks and under the horses' bellies. I'll turn some of 'em on to you, my boy, and then you'll know a little more about it."

Well, all this puzzled me a good deal, as you can imagine, Bertie; for, making every allowance for Cullingworth's inflated way of talking, there must be something at the back of it. I was thinking to myself that I must keep my head cool, and have a look at everything with my own eyes, when the carriage pulled up and we got out.

"This is my little place," said Cullingworth.

It was the corner house of a line of fine buildings, and looked to me much more like a good-sized hotel than a private mansion. It had a broad sweep of steps leading to the door, and towered away up to five or six stories, with pinnacles and a flagstaff on the top. As a matter of fact, I learned that before Cullingworth took it, it had been one of the chief clubs in the town, but the committee had abandoned it on account of the heavy rent. A smart maid opened the door; and a moment later I was shaking hands with Mrs. Cullingworth, who was all kindliness and cordiality. She has, I think, forgotten the little Avonmouth business, when her husband and I fell out.

The inside of the house was even huger than I had thought from the look of the exterior. There were over thirty bedrooms, Cullingworth informed me, as he helped me to carry my portmanteau upstairs. The hall and first stair were most excellently furnished and carpeted, but it all run to nothing at the landing. My own bedroom had a little iron bed, and a small basin standing on a packing case. Cullingworth took a hammer from the mantelpiece, and began to knock in nails behind the door.

"These will do to hang your clothes on," said he; "you don't mind roughing it a little until we get things in order?"

"Not in the least."

"You see," he explained, "there's no good my putting a forty pound suite into a bed-room, and then having to chuck it all out of the window in order to make room for a hundred-pound one. No sense in that, Munro! Eh, what! I'm going to furnish this house as no house has ever been furnished. By Crums! I'll bring the folk from a hundred miles round just to have leave to look at it. But I must do it room by room. Come down with me and look at the dining-room. You must be hungry after your journey."

It really was furnished in a marvellous way - nothing flash, and everything magnificent. The carpet was so rich that my feet seemed to sink into it as into deep moss. The soup was on the table, and Mrs. Cullingworth sitting down, but he kept hauling me round to look at something else.

"Go on, Hetty," he cried over his shoulder. "I just want to show Munro this. Now, these plain dining-room chairs, what d'you think they cost each? Eh, what?"

"Five pounds," said I at a venture.

"Exactly!" he cried, in great delight; "thirty pounds for the six. You hear, Hetty! Munro guessed the price first shot. Now, my boy, what for the pair of curtains?"

They were a magnificent pair of stamped crimson velvet, with a two-foot gilt cornice above them. I thought that I had better not imperil my newly gained reputation by guessing.

"Eighty pounds!" he roared, slapping them with the back of his hand. "Eighty pounds, Munro! What d'ye think of that? Everything that I have in this house is going to be of the best. Why, look at this waiting-aid! Did you ever see a neater one?"

He swung the girl, towards me by the arm.

Don't be silly, Jimmy," said Mrs. Cullingworth mildly, while he roared with laughter, with all his fangs flashing under his bristling moustache. The girl edged closer to her mistress, looking half-frightened and half-angry.

"All right, Mary, no harm!" he cried. "Sit down, Munro, old chap. Get a bottle of champagne, Mary, and we'll drink to more luck."

Well, we had a very pleasant little dinner. It is never slow if Cullingworth is about. He is one of those men who make a kind of magnetic atmosphere, so that you feel exhilarated and stimulated in their presence. His mind is so nimble and his thoughts so extravagant, that your own break away from their usual grooves, and surprise you by their activity. You feel pleased at your own inventiveness and originality, when you are really like the wren when it took a lift on the eagle's shoulder. Old Peterson, you remember, used to have a similar effect upon you in the Linlithgow days.

In the middle of dinner he plunged off, and came back with a round bag about the size of a pomegranate in his hand.

"What d'ye think this is, Munro? Eh?"

"I have no idea."

"Our day's take. Eh, Hetty?" He undid a string, and in an instant a pile of gold and silver rattled down upon the cloth, the coins whirling and clinking among the dishes. One rolled off the table and was retrieved by the maid from some distant corner.

"What is it, Mary? A half sovereign? Put it in your pocket. What did the lot come to, Hetty?"

"Thirty-one pound eight."

"You see, Munro! One day's work." He plunged his hand into his trouser pocket and brought out a pile of sovereigns, which he balanced in his palm. "Look at that, laddie. Rather different from my Avonmouth form, eh? What?"

"It will be good news for them," I suggested.

He was scowling at me in an instant with all his old ferocity. You cannot imagine a more savage-looking creature than Cullingworth is when his temper goes wrong. He gets a perfectly fiendish expression in his light blue eyes, and all his hair bristles up like a striking cobra. He isn't a beauty at his best, but at his worst he's really phenomenal. At the first danger signal his wife had ordered the maid from the room.

"What rot you do talk, Munro!" he cried. "Do you suppose I am going to cripple myself for years by letting those debts hang on to me?"

"I understood that you had promised," said I. "Still, of course, it is no business of mine."

"I should hope not," he cried. "A tradesman stands to win or to lose. He allows a margin for bad debts. I would have paid it if I could. I couldn't, and so I wiped the slate clean. No one in his senses would dream of spending all the money that I make in Bradfield upon the tradesmen of Avonmouth."

"Suppose they come down upon you?"

"Well, we'll see about that when they do. Meanwhile I am paying ready money for every mortal thing that comes up the door steps. They think so well of me here that I could have had the whole place furnished like a palace from the drain pipes to the flagstaff, only I determined to take each room in turn when I was ready for it. There's nearly four hundred pounds under this one ceiling."

There came a tap at the door, and in walked a boy in buttons.

"If you please, sir, Mr. Duncan wishes to see you."

"Give my compliments to Mr. Duncan, and tell him he may go to the devil!"

"My dear Jimmy!" cried Mrs. Cullingworth.

"Tell him I am at dinner; and if all the kings in Europe were waiting in the hall with their crowns in their hands I wouldn't cross that door mat to see them."

The boy vanished, but was back in an instant.

"Please, sir, he won't go."

"Won't go! What d'you mean?" Cullingworth sat with his mouth open and his knife and fork sticking up. "What d'you mean, you brat? What are you boggling about?"

"It's his bill, sir," said the frightened boy.

Cullingworth's face grew dusky, and the veins began to swell on his forehead.

"His bill, eh! Look here!" He took his watch out and laid it on the table. "It's two minutes to eight. At eight I'm coming out, and if I find him there I'll strew the street with him. Tell him I'll shred him over the parish. He has two minutes to save his life in, and one of them is nearly gone."

The boy bolted from the room, and in an instant afterwards we heard the bang of the front door, with a clatter of steps down the stairs. Cullingworth lay back in his chair and roared until the tears shone on his eyelashes, while his wife quivered all over with sympathetic merriment.

"I'll drive him mad," Cullingworth sobbed at last. "He's a nervous, chicken-livered kind of man; and when I look at him he turns the colour of putty. If I pass his shop I usually just drop in and stand and loo at him. I never speak, but just look. It paralyses him. Sometimes the shop is full of people; but it is just the same."

"Who is he, then?" I asked.

"He's my corn merchant. I was saying that I paid my tradesmen as I go, but he is the only exception. He has done me once or twice, you see; and so I try to take it out of him. By the way, you might send him down twenty pounds to-morrow, Hetty. It's time for an instalment."

What a gossip you will think me, Bertie? But when I begin, my memory brings everything back so clearly, and I write on and on almost unconsciously. Besides, this fellow is such a mixture of qualities, that I could never give you any idea of him by myself; and so I just try to repeat to you what he says, and what he does, so that you may build up your own picture of the man. I know that he has always interested you, and that he does so more now than ever since our fates have drawn us together again.

After dinner, we went into the back room, which was the most extraordinary contrast to the front one, having only a plain deal table, and half-a-dozen kitchen chairs scattered about on a linoleum floor. At one end was an electric battery and a big magnet. At the other, a packing case with several pistols and a litter of cartridges upon it. A rook rifle was leaning tip against it, and looking round I saw that the walls were all pocked with bullet marks.

"What's this, then?" I asked, rolling my eyes round.

"Hetty, what's this?" he asked, with his pipe in his hand and his head cocked sideways.

"Naval supremacy and the command of the seas," said she, like a child repeating a lesson.

"That's it he shouted, stabbing at me with the amber. "Naval supremacy and command of the seas. It's all here right under your nose. I tell you, Munro, I could go to Switzerland to-morrow, and I could say to them - `Look here, you haven't got a seaboard and you haven't got a port; but just find me a ship, and hoist your flag on it, and I'll give you every ocean under heaven.' I'd sweep the seas until there wasn't a match-box floating on them. Or I could make them over to a limited company, and join the board after allotment. I hold the salt water in the cup of this hand, every drop of it."

His wife put her hands on his shoulder with admiration in her eyes. I turned to knock out my pipe, and grinned over the grate.

"Oh, you may grin," said he. (He was wonderfully quick at spotting what you were doing.) "You'll grin a

Sir A. C. Doyle

little wider when you see the dividends coming in. What's the value of that magnet?"

"A pound?"

"A million pounds. Not a penny under. And dirt cheap to the nation that buys it. I shall let it go at that, though I could make ten times as much if I held on. I shall take it up to the Secretary of the Navy in a week or two; and if he seems to be a civil deserving sort of person I shall do business with him. It's not every day, Munro, that a man comes into his office with the Atlantic under one arm and the Pacific under the other. Eh, what?"

I knew it would make him savage, but I lay back in my chair and laughed until I was tired. His wife looked at me reproachfully; but he, after a moment of blackness, burst out laughing also, stamping up and down the room and waving his arms.

"Of course it seems absurd to you," he cried. "Well, I daresay it would to me if any other fellow had worked it out. But you may take my word for it that it's all right. Hetty here will answer for it. Won't you, Hetty?"

"It's splendid, my dear."

"Now I'll show you, Munro; what an unbelieving Jew you are, trying to look interested, and giggling at the back of your throat! In the first place, I have discovered a method - which I won't tell you - of increasing the attractive power of a magnet a hundredfold. Have you grasped that?"

"Yes."

"Very good. You are also aware, I presume, that modern projectiles are either made of or tipped with steel. It may possibly have come to your ears that magnets attract steel. Permit me now to show you a small experiment." He bent over his apparatus, and I suddenly heard the snapping of electricity. "This," he continued going across to the packing case, "is a saloon pistol, and will be exhibited in the museums of the next century as being the weapon with which the new era was inaugurated. Into the breech I place a Boxer cartridge, specialty provided for experimental purposes with a steel bullet. I aim point blank at the dab of red sealing wax upon the wall, which is four inches above the magnet. I am an absolutely dead shot. I fire. You will now advance, and satisfy yourself that the bullet is flattened upon the end of the magnet, after which you will apologise to me for that grin."

I looked, and it certainly was as he had said.

"I'll tell you what I would do," he cried. "I am prepared to put that magnet in Hetty's bonnet, and to let you fire six shots straight at her face. How's that for a test? You wouldn't mind, Hetty? Eh, what!"

"I don't think she would have objected, but I hastened to disclaim any share in such an experiment.

"Of course, you see that the whole thing is to scale. My warship of the future carries at her prow and stern a magnet which shall be as much larger than that as the big shell will be larger than this tiny bullet. Or I might have a separate raft, possibly, to carry my apparatus. My ship goes into action. What happens then, Munro? Eh, what! Every shot fired at her goes smack on to the magnet. There's a reservoir below into which they drop when the electric circuit is broken. After every action they are sold by auction for old metal, and the result divided as prize money among the crew. But think of it, man! I tell you it is an absolute impossibility for a shot to strike any ship which is provided with my apparatus. And then look at the cheapness. You don't want armour. You want nothing. Any ship that floats becomes invulnerable with one of these. The war ship of the future will cost anything from seven pound ten. You're grinning again; but if you give me a magnet and a Brixton trawler with a seven-pounder gun I'll show sport to the finest battle-ship afloat."

"Well, there must be some flaw about this," I suggested. "If your magnet is so strong as all that, you would have your own broadside boomeranging back upon you."

"Not a bit of it! There's a big difference between a shot flying away from you with all its muzzle velocity, and another one which is coming towards you and only needs a slight deflection to strike the magnet. Besides, by breaking the circuit I can take off the influence when I am firing my own broadside. Then I connect, and instantly become invulnerable."

"And your nails and screws?"

"The warship of the future will be bolted together by wood."

Well, he would talk of nothing else the whole evening but of this wonderful invention of his. Perhaps there is nothing in it - probably there is not; and yet it illustrates the many-sided nature of the man, that he should not say one word about his phenominal success here - of which I am naturally most anxious to hear - not a word either upon the important subject of our partnership, but will think and talk of nothing but this extraordinary naval idea. In a week he will have tossed it aside in all probability, and be immersed in some plan for reuniting the Jews and settling them in Madagascar. Yet from all he has said, and all I have seen, there can be no doubt that he has in some inexplicable way made a tremendous hit, and to-morrow I shall let you know all about it. Come what may, I am delighted that I came, for things promise to be interesting. Regard this not as the end of a letter, but of a paragraph. You shall have the conclusion to-morrow, or on Thursday at the latest. Goodbye, and my remembrance to Lawrence if you see him. How's your friend from Yale?

VII.

1 THE PARADE, BRADFIELD,
9th March, 1882.

Well, you see I am as good as my word, Bertie; and here is a full account of this queer little sample gouged out of real life, never to be seen, I should fancy, by any eye save your own. I have written to Horton also, and of course to my mother; but I don't go into detail with them, as I have got into the way of doing with you. You keep on assuring me that you like it; so on your own head be it if you find my experiences gradually developing into a weariness.

When I woke in the morning, and looked round at the bare walls and the basin on the packing case, I hardly knew where I was. Cullingworth came charging into the room in his dressing gown, however, and roused me effectually by putting his hands on the rail at the end of the bed, and throwing a somersault over it which brought his heels on to my pillow with a thud. He was in great spirits, and, squatting on the bed, he held forth about his plans while I dressed.

"I tell you one of the first things I mean to do, Munro," said he. "I mean to have a paper of my own. We'll start a weekly paper here, you and I, and we'll make them sit up all round. We'll have an organ of our own, just like every French politician. If any one crosses us, we'll make them wish they had never been born. Eh, what, laddie? what d'you think? So clever, Munro, that everybody's bound to read it, and so scathing that it will just fetch out blisters every time. Don't you think we could?"

"What politics?" I asked.

"Oh, curse the politics! Red pepper well rubbed in, that's my idea of a paper. Call it the Scorpion. Chaff the Mayor and the Council until they call a meeting and hang themselves. I'd do the snappy paragraphs, and you would do the fiction and poetry. I thought about it during the night, and Hetty has written to Murdoch's to get an estimate for the printing. We might get our first number out this day week."

"My dear chap!" I gasped.

"I want you to start a novel this morning. You won't get many patients at first, and you'll have lots of time."

"But I never wrote a line in my life."

"A properly balanced man can do anything he sets his hand to. He's got every possible quality inside him, and all he wants is the will to develop it."

"Could you write a novel yourself?" I asked.

"Of course I could. Such a novel, Munro, that when they'd read the first chapter the folk would just sit groaning until the second came out. They'd wait in rows outside my door in the hope of hearing what was coming next. By Crums, I'll go and begin it now! "And, with another somersault over the end of the bed, he rushed from the room, with the tassels of his dressing gown flying behind him.

I daresay you've quite come to the conclusion by this time that Cullingworth is simply an interesting pathological study - a man in the first stage of lunacy or general paralysis. You might not be so sure about it if you were in close contact with him. He justifies his wildest flights by what he does. It sounds grotesque when put down in black and white; but then it would have sounded equally grotesque a year ago if he had said that he would build up a huge practice in a twelvemonth. Now we see that he has done it. His possibilities are immense. He has such huge energy at the back of his fertility of invention. I am afraid, on thinking over all that I have written to you, that I may have given you a false impression of the man by dwelling too much on those incidents in which he has shown the strange and violent side of his character, and omitting the stretches between where his wisdom and judgment have had a chance. His conversation when he does not fly off at a tangent is full of pith and idea. "The greatest monument ever erected to Napoleon Buonaparte was the British National debt," said he yesterday. Again, "We must never forget that the principal export of Great Britain to the United States IS the United States." Again, speaking of Christianity, "What is intellectually unsound cannot be morally sound." He shoots off a whole column of aphorisms in a single evening. I should like to have a man with a note book always beside him to gather up his waste. No; you must not let me give you a false impression of the man's capacity. On the other hand, it would be dishonest to deny that I think him thoroughly unscrupulous, and full of very sinister traits. I am much mistaken, however, if he has not fine strata in his nature. He is capable of rising to heights as well as of sinking to depths.

Well, when we had breakfasted we got into the carriage and drove off to the place of business.

"I suppose you are surprised at Hetty coming with us, said Cullingworth, slapping me on the knee. Hetty, Munro is wondering what the devil you are here for, only he is too polite to ask."

In fact, it HAD struck me as rather strange that she should, as a matter of course, accompany us to business.

"You'll see when we get there," he cried chuckling. "We run this affair on lines of our own."

It was not very far, and we soon found ourselves outside a square whitewashed building, which had a huge "Dr. Cullingworth" on a great brass plate at the side of the door. Underneath was printed "May be consulted gratis from ten to four." The door was open, and I caught a glimpse of a crowd of people waiting in the hall.

"How many here?" asked Cullingworth of the page boy.

"A hundred and forty, sir."

"All the waiting rooms full?"

"Yes, sir."

"Courtyard full?

"Yes, sir."

"Stable full?"

"Yes, sir."

"Coach-house full?"

"There's still room in the coach-house, sir."

"Ah, I'm sorry we haven't got a crowded day for you, Munro," said he. "Of course, we can't command these things, and must take them as they come. Now then, now then, make a gangway, can't you?" - this to his patients. "Come here and see the waiting-room. Pooh! what an atmosphere! Why on earth can't you open the windows for yourselves? I never saw such folk! There are thirty people in this room, Munro, and not one with sense enough to open a window to save himself from suffocation."

"I tried, sir, but there's a screw through the sash," cried one fellow.

"Ah, my boy, you'll never get on in the world if you can't open a window without raising a sash," said Cullingworth, slapping him on the shoulder. He took the man's umbrella and stuck it through two of the panes of glass.

"That's the way!" he said. "Boy, see that the screw is taken out. Now then, Munro, come along, and we'll get to work."

We went up a wooden stair, uncarpeted, leaving every room beneath us, as far as I could see, crowded with patients. At the top was a bare passage, which had two rooms opposite to each other at one end, and a single one at the other.

"This is my consulting room," said he, leading the way into one of these. It was a good-sized square chamber, perfectly empty save for two plain wooden chairs and an unpainted table with two books and a stethoscope upon it. "It doesn't look like four or five thousand a year, does it? Now, there is an exactly similar one opposite which you can have for yourself. I'll send across any surgical cases which may turn up. To-day, however, I think you had better stay with me, and see how I work things."

"I should very much like to," said I.

"There are one or two elementary rules to be observed in the way of handling patients," he remarked, seating himself on the table and swinging his legs. "The most obvious is that you must never let them see that you want them. It should be pure condescension on your part seeing them at all; and the more difficulties you throw in the way of it, the more they think of it. Break your patients in early, and keep them well to heel. Never make the fatal mistake of being polite to them. Many foolish young men fall into this habit, and are ruined in consequence. Now, this is my form" - he sprang to the door, and putting his two hands to his mouth he bellowed: "Stop your confounded jabbering down there! I might as well be living above a poultry show! There, you see," he added to me, "they will think ever so much more of me for that."

"But don't they get offended?" I asked.

"I'm afraid not. I have a name for this sort of thing now, and they have come to expect it. But an offended patient - I mean a thoroughly insulted one - is the finest advertisement in the world. If it is a woman, she runs clacking about among her friends until your name becomes a household word, and they all pretend to sympathise with her, and agree among themselves that you must be a remarkably discerning man. I quarrelled with one man about the state of his gall duct, and it ended by my throwing him down the stairs. What was the result? He talked so much about it that the whole village from which he came, sick and well, trooped to see me. The little country practitioner who had been buttering them up for a quarter of a century found that he might as well put up his shutters. It's human nature, my boy, and you can't alter it. Eh, what? You make yourself cheap and you become cheap. You put a high price on yourself and they rate you at that price. Suppose I set up in Harley Street to-morrow, and made it all nice and easy, with hours from ten to three, do you think I should get a patient? I might starve first. How would I work it? I should let it be known that I only saw patients from midnight until two in the morning, and that bald-headed people must pay double. That would set people talking, their curiosity would be stimulated, and in four months the street would be blocked all night. Eh, what? laddie, you'd go yourself. That's my principle here. I often come in of a morning and send them all about their business, tell them I'm going off to the country for a day. I turn away forty pounds, and it's worth four hundred as an advertisement!"

"But I understood from the plate that the consultations were gratis."

"So they are, but they have to pay for the medicine. And if a patient wishes to come out of turn he has to pay half-a-guinea for the privilege. There are generally about twenty every day who would rather pay that than wait several hours. But, mind you, Munro, don't you make any mistake about this! All this would go for nothing if you had not something, slid behind - I cure them. That's the point. I take cases that others have despaired of, and I cure them right off. All the rest is only to bring them here. But once here I keep them on my merits. It would all be a flash in the pan but for that. Now, come along and see Hetty's department."

We walked down the passage to the other room. It was elaborately fitted up as a dispensary, and there with a chic little apron Mrs. Cullingworth was busy making up pills. With her sleeves turned up and a litter of glasses and bottles all round her, she was laughing away like a little child among its toys.

"The best dispenser in the world!" cried Cullingworth, patting her on the shoulder. "You see how I do it, Munro. I write on a label what the prescription is, and make a sign which shows how much is to be charged. The man comes along the passage and passes the label through the pigeon hole. Hetty makes it up, passes out the bottle, and takes the money. Now, come on and clear some of these folk out of the house."

It is impossible for me to give you any idea of that long line of patients, filing hour after hour through the unfurnished room, and departing, some amused, and some frightened, with their labels in their hands. Cullingworth's antics are beyond belief. I laughed until I thought the wooden chair under me would have come to pieces. He roared, he raved, he swore, he pushed them about, slapped them on the back, shoved them against the wall, and occasionally rushed out to the head of the stair to address them en masse. At the same time, behind all this tomfoolery, I, watching his prescriptions, could see a quickness of diagnosis, a scientific insight, and a daring and unconventional use of drugs, which satisfied me that he was right in saying that, under all this charlatanism, there lay solid reasons for his success. Indeed, "charlatanism" is a misapplied word in this connection; for it would describe the doctor who puts on an artificial and conventional manner with his patients, rather than one who is absolutely frank and true to his own extraordinary nature.

To some of his patients he neither said one word nor did he allow them to say one. With a loud "hush" he would rush at them, thump them on the chests, listen to their hearts, write their labels, and then run them out of the room by their shoulders. One poor old lady he greeted with a perfect scream. "You've been drinking too much tea!" he cried. "You are suffering from tea poisoning!" Then, without allowing her to get a word in, he clutched her by her crackling black mantle, dragged her up to the table, and held out a copy of "Taylor's Medical Jurisprudence" which was lying there. "Put your hand on the book," he thundered, "and swear that for fourteen days you will drink nothing but cocoa." She swore with upturned eyes, and was instantly whirled off with her label in her hand, to the dispensary. I could imagine that to the last day of her life, the old lady would talk of her interview with Cullingworth; and I could well understand how the village from which she came would send fresh recruits to block up his waiting rooms.

Another portly person was seized by the two armholes of his waistcoat, just as he was opening his mouth to explain his symptoms, and was rushed backward down the passage, down the stairs, and finally into the street, to the immense delight of the assembled patients, "You eat too much, drink too much, and sleep too much," Cullingworth roared after him. "Knock down a policeman, and come again when they let you out." Another patient complained of a "sinking feeling." "My dear," said he, "take your medicine; and if that does no good, swallow the cork, for there is nothing better when you are sinking."

As far as I could judge, the bulk of the patients looked upon a morning at Cullingworth's as a most enthralling public entertainment, tempered only by a thrill lest it should be their turn next to be made an exhibition of.

Well, with half-an-hour for lunch, this extraordinary business went on till a quarter to four in the afternoon. When the last patient had departed, Cullingworth led the way into the dispensary, where all the fees had been arranged upon the counter in the order of their value. There were seventeen half-sovereigns, seventy-three shillings, and forty-six florins; or thirty-two pounds eight and sixpence in all. Cullingworth counted it up, and then mixing the gold and silver into one heap, he sat running his fingers through it and playing with it. Finally, he raked it into the canvas bag which I had seen the night before, and lashed the neck up with a boot-lace.

We walked home, and that walk struck me as the most extraordinary part of all that extraordinary day. Cullingworth paraded slowly through the principal treets with his canvas bag, full of money, outstretched at the full length of his arm. His wife and I walked on either side, like two acolytes supporting a priest, and so we made our way solemnly homewards the people stopping to see us pass.

"I always make a point of walking through the doctor's quarter," said Cullingworth. "We are passing through it now. They all come to their windows and gnash their teeth and dance until I am out of sight."

"Why should you quarrel with them? What is the matter with them?" I asked.

"Pooh! what's the use of being mealy-mouthed about it?" said he. "We are all trying to cut each other's throats, and why should we be hypocritical over it? They haven't got a good word for me, any one of them; so I like to take a rise out of them."

"I must say that I can see no sense in that. They are your brothers in the profession, with the same education and the same knowledge. Why should you take an offensive attitude towards them?"

"That's what I say, Dr. Munro," cried his wife. "It is so very unpleasant to feel that one is surrounded by enemies on every side."

"Hetty's riled because their wives wouldn't call upon her," he cried. "Look at that, my dear," jingling his bag. "That is better than having a lot of brainless women drinking tea and cackling in our drawing-room. I've had a big card printed, Munro, saying that we don't desire to increase the circle of our acquaintance. The maid has orders to show it to every suspicious person who calls."

"Why should you not make money at your practice, and yet remain on good terms with your professional brethren?" said I. "You speak as if the two things were incompatible."

"So they are. What's the good of beating about the bush, laddie? My methods are all unprofessional, and I break every law of medical etiquette as often as I can think of it. You know very well that the British Medical Association would hold up their hands in horror if it could see what you have seen to-day."

"But why not conform to professional etiquette?"

"Because I know better. My boy, I'm a doctor's son, and I've seen too much of it. I was born inside the machine, and I've seen all the wires. All this etiquette is a dodge for keeping the business in the hands of the older men. It's to hold the young men back, and to stop the holes by which they might slip through to the front. I've heard my father say so a score of times. He had the largest practice in Scotland, and yet he was absolutely devoid of brains. He slipped into it through seniority and decorum. No pushing, but take your turn. Very well, laddie, when you're at the top of the line, but how about it when you've just taken your place at the tail? When I'm on the top rung I shall look down and say, `Now, you youngsters, we are going to have very strict etiquette, and I beg that you will come up very quietly and not disarrange me from my comfortable position.' At the same time, if they do what I tell them, I shall look upon them as a lot of infernal blockheads. Eh, Munro, what?"

I could only say again that I thought he took a very low view of the profession, and that I disagreed with every word he said.

"Well, my boy, you may disagree as much as you like, but if you are going to work with me you must throw etiquette to the devil!"

"I can't do that."

"Well, if you are too clean handed for the job you can clear out. We can't keep you here against your will."

I said nothing; but when we got back, I went upstairs and packed up my trunk, with every intention of going back to Yorkshire by the night train. He came up to my room, and finding what I was at, he burst into apologies which would have satisfied a more exacting man than I am.

"You shall do just exactly what you like, my dear chap. If you don't like my way, you may try some way of your own."

"That's fair enough," said I. "But it's a little trying to a man's self-respect if he is told to clear out every time there is a difference of opinion."

"Well, well, there was no harm meant, and it shan't occur again. I can't possibly say more than that; so come along down and have a cup of tea."

And so the matter blew over; but I very much fear, Bertie, that this is the first row of a series. I have a presentiment that sooner or later my position here will become untenable. Still, I shall give it a fair trial as long as he will let me. Cullingworth is a fellow who likes to have nothing but inferiors and dependants round him. Now, I like to stand on my own legs, and think with my own mind. If he'll let me do this we'll get along very well; but if I know the man he will claim submission, which is more than I am inclined to give. He has a right to my gratitude, which I freely admit. He has found an opening for me when I badly needed one and had no immediate prospects. But still, one may pay too high a price even for that, and I should feel that I was doing so if I had to give up my individuality and my manhood.

We had an incident that evening which was so characteristic that I must tell you of it. Cullingworth has an air gun which fires little steel darts. With this he makes excellent practice at about twenty feet, the length of the back room. We were shooting at a mark after dinner, when he asked me whether I would hold a halfpenny between my finger and thumb, and allow him to shoot it out. A halfpenny not being forthcoming, he took a bronze medal out of his waistcoat pocket, and I held that tip as a mark. Kling!" went the air gun, and the medal rolled upon the floor.

"Plumb in the centre," said he.

"On the contrary," I answered, "you never hit it at all!"

"Never hit it! I must have hit it!"

"I am confident you didn't."

"Where's the dart, then?"

"Here," said I, holding up a bleeding forefinger, from which the tail end of the fluff with which the dart was winged was protruding.

I never saw a man so abjectly sorry for anything in my life. He used language of self-reproach which would have been extravagant if he had shot off one of my limbs. Our positions were absurdly reversed; and it was he who sat collapsed in a chair, while it was I, with the dart still in my finger, who leaned over him and laughed the matter off. Mrs. Cullingworth had run for hot water, and presently with a tweezers we got the intruder out. There was very little pain (more to-day than yesterday), but if ever you are called upon to identify my body you may look for a star at the end of my right forefinger.

When the surgery was completed (Cullingworth writhing and groaning all the time) my eyes happened to catch the medal which I had dropped, lying upon the carpet. I lifted it up and looked at it, eager to find some topic which would be more agreeable. Printed upon it was - "Presented to James Cullingworth for gallantry in saving life. Jan. 1879."

"Hullo, Cullingworth," said I. "You never told me about this!"

He was off in an instant in his most extravagant style.

"What! the medal? Haven't you got one? I thought every one had. You prefer to be select, I suppose. It was a little boy. You've no idea the trouble I had to get him in."

"Get him out, you mean."

"My dear chap, you don't understand! Any one could get a child out. It's getting one in that's the bother. One deserves a medal for it. Then there are the witnesses, four shillings a day I had to pay them, and a quart of beer in the evenings. You see you can't pick up a child and carry it to the edge of a pier and throw it in. You'd have all sorts of complications with the parents. You must be patient and wait until you get a legitimate chance. I caught a quinsy walking up and down Avonmouth pier before I saw my opportunity. He was rather a stolid fat boy, and he was sitting on the very edge, fishing. I got the sole of my foot on to the small of his back, and shot him an incredible distance. I had some little difficulty in getting him out, for his fishing line got twice round my legs, but it all ended well, and the witnesses were as staunch as possible. The boy came up to thank me next day, and said that he was quite uninjured save for a bruise on the back. His parents always send me a brace of fowls every Christmas."

I was sitting with my finger in the hot water listening to this rigmarole. When he had finished he ran off to get his tobacco box, and we could hear the bellowing of his laughter dwindling up the stair. I was still looking at the medal, which, from the dents all over it, had evidently been often used as a target, when I felt a timid touch upon my sleeve; it was Mrs. Cullingworth, who was looking earnestly at me with a very distressed expression upon her face.

"You believe far too much what James says," said she. "You don't know him in the least, Mr. Munro. You don't look at a thing from his point of view, and you will never understand him until you do. It is not, of course, that he means to say anything that is untrue; but his fancy is excited, and he is quite carried away by the humour of any idea, whether it tells against himself or not. It hurts me, Mr. Munro, to see the only man in the world towards whom he has any feeling of friendship, misunderstanding him so completely, for very often when you say nothing your face shows very clearly what you think."

I could only answer lamely that I was very sorry if I had misjudged her husband in any way, and that no one had a keener appreciation of some of his qualities than I had.

"I saw how gravely you looked when he told you that absurd story about pushing a little boy into the water," she continued; and, as she spoke, she drew from somewhere in the front of her dress a much creased slip of paper. "Just glance at that, please, Dr. Munro."

It was a newspaper cutting, which gave the true account of the incident. Suffice it that it was an ice accident, and that Cullingworth had really behaved in a heroic way and had been drawn out himself insensible, with the child so clasped in his arms that it was not until he had recovered his senses that they were able to separate them. I had hardly finished reading it when we heard his step on the stairs; and she, thrusting the paper back into her bosom, became in an instant the same silently watchful woman as ever.

Is he not a conundrum? If he interests you at a distance (and I take for granted that what you say in your letters is not merely conventional compliment) you can think how piquant he is in actual life. I must confess, however, that I can never shake off the feeling that I am living with some capricious creature who frequently growls and may possibly bite. Well, it won't be very long before I write again, and by that time I shall probably know whether I am likely to find any permanent billet here or not. I am so sorry to hear about Mrs. Swanborough's indisposition. You know that I take the deepest interest in everything that affects you. They tell me here that I am looking very fit, though I think they ought to spell it with an "a."

VIII.

1 THE PARADE, BRADFIELD,
6th April, 1882.

I am writing this, my dear Bertie, at a little table which
has been fitted up in the window of my bedroom.Every
one in the house is asleep except myself; and all the
noise of the city is hushed. Yet my own brain is
singularly active, and I feel that I am better employed
in sitting up and writing to you, than in tossing about
upon my bed. I am often accused of being sleepy in the
daytime, but every now and then Nature gets level by
making me abnormally wakeful at night.

Are you conscious of the restful influence which the
stars exert? To me they are the most soothing things in
Nature. I am proud to say that I don't know the name
of one of them. The glamour and romance would pass
away from them if they were all classified and ticketed
in one's brain. But when a man is hot and flurried, and
full of his own little ruffled dignities and infinitesimal
misfortunes, then a star bath is the finest thing in the
world. They are so big, and so serene and so lovely.
They tell me that the interplanetary spaces are full of
the debris of shattered asteroids; so, perhaps, even
among them there are such things as disease and death.
Yet just to look at them must remind a man of what a
bacillus of a thing he is - the whole human race like
some sprinkling of impalpable powder upon the

surface of one of the most insignificant fly-wheels of a monstrous machine. But there's order in it, Bertie, there's order! And where there is order there must be mind, and where there is mind there must be sense of Justice. I don't allow that there can be any doubt as to the existence of that central Mind, or as to the possession by it of certain attributes. The stars help me to realise these. It is strange, when one looks upon them, to think that the Churches are still squabbling down here over such questions as whether the Almighty is most gratified by our emptying a tea-spoonful of water over our babies' heads, or by our waiting a few years and then plunging them bodily into a tank. It would be comic if it were not so tragic.

This train of thought is the after-swell from an argument with Cullingworth this evening. He holds that the human race is deteriorating mentally and morally. He calls out at the grossness which confounds the Creator with a young Jewish Philosopher. I tried to show him that this is no proof of degeneration, since the Jewish Philosopher at least represented a moral idea, and was therefore on an infinitely higher plane than the sensual divinities of the ancients. His own views of the Creator seem to me to be a more evident degeneration. He declares that looking round at Nature he can see nothing but ruthlessness and brutality. "Either the Creator is not all-powerful, or else He is not all-good," says he. "Either He can stop these atrocities and won't, in which case He is not all-good; or else He would stop them but can't, in which case He is not all-powerful." It was a difficult dilemma for a man who professes to stick to reason to get out of. Of course, if you plead faith, you can always slip out of anything. I was forced to get behind a corner of that buckler with which you have so often turned my own

Sir A. C. Doyle

thrusts. I said that the dilemma arose from our taking it for granted that that which seemed evil really was EVIL. "It lies with you to prove that it isn't," said he. "We may hope that it isn't," said I. "Wait until some one tells you that you have cancer of the pyloric end of the stomach," said he; and he shouted it out again every time I tried to renew the argument.

But in all soberness, I really do think, Bertie, that very much which seems to be saddest in life might be very different if we could focus it properly. I tried to give you my views about this in the case of drink and immorality. But physically, I fancy that it applies more obviously than it does morally. All the physical evils of life seem to culminate in death; and yet death, as I have seen it, has not been a painful or terrible process. In many cases, a man dies without having incurred nearly as much pain, during the whole of his fatal illness, as would have arisen from a whitlow or an abscess of the jaw. And it is often those deaths which seem most terrible to the onlooker, which are least so to the sufferer. When a man is overtaken by an express and shivered into fragments, or when he drops from a fourth-floor window and is smashed into a bag of splinters, the unfortunate spectators are convulsed with horror, and find a text for pessimistic views about the Providence which allows such things to be. And yet, it is very doubtful whether the deceased, could his tongue be loosened, would remember anything at all about the matter. We know, as students of medicine, that though pain is usually associated with cancers and with abdominal complaints; still, in the various fevers, in apoplexy, in blood poisonings, in lung diseases, and, in short, in the greater proportion of serious maladies, there is little suffering.

I remember how struck I was when first I saw the actual cautery applied in a case of spinal disease. The white hot iron was pressed firmly into the patient's back, without the use of any anaesthetic, and what with the sight and the nauseating smell of burned flesh I felt faint and ill. Yet, to my astonishment, the patient never flinched nor moved a muscle of his face, and on my inquiring afterwards, he assured me that the proceeding was absolutely painless, a remark which was corroborated by the surgeon. "The nerves are so completely and instantaneously destroyed," he explained, "that they have no time to convey a painful impression." But then if this be so, what becomes of all the martyrs at the stake, and the victims of Red Indians, and other poor folk over whose sufferings and constancy we have wondered? It may be that Providence is not only not cruel itself, but will not allow man to be cruel either. Do your worst, and it will step in with a "No, I won't allow this poor child of mine to be hurt"; and then comes the dulling of the nerve and the lethargy which takes the victim out of the reach of the tormentor. David Livingstone under the claws of the lion must have looked like an object lesson of the evil side of things, and yet he has left it upon record that his own sensations were pleasurable rather than otherwise. I am well convinced that if the newly-born infant and the man who had just died could compare their experiences, the former would have proved to be the sufferer. It is not for nothing that the first thing the newcomer into this planet does is to open its toothless mouth and protest energetically against fate.

Cullingworth has written a parable which makes a paragraph for our wonderful new weekly paper.

"The little cheese mites held debate," he says,"as to who made the cheese. Some thought that they had no data to go upon, and some that it had come together by a solidification of vapour, or by the centrifugal attraction of atoms. A few surmised that the platter might have something to do with it; but the wisest of them could not deduce the existence of a cow."

We are at one, he and I, in thinking that the infinite is beyond our perception. We differ only in that he sees evil and I see good in the working of the universe. Ah, what a mystery it all is! Let us be honest and humble and think kindly of each other. There's a line of stars all winking at me over the opposite roof - winking slyly at the silly little person with the pen and paper who is so earnest about what he can never understand.

Well, now, I'll come back to something practical. It is nearly a month since I wrote to you last. The date is impressed upon my memory because it was the day after Cullingworth shot the air-dart into my finger. The place festered and prevented my writing to any one for a week or two, but it is all right again now. I have ever so much of different sorts to tell you, but really when I come to think of it, it does not amount to very much after all.

First of all, about the practice. I told you that I was to have a room immediately opposite to Cullingworth's, and that all the surgical cases were to be turned over to me. For a few days I had nothing to do, except to listen to him romping and scuffling with his patients, or making speeches to them from the top of the stairs. However, a great "Dr. Stark Munro, Surgeon," has been affixed to the side of the door downstairs, opposite Cullingworth's plate; and a proud man was I when first my eyes lit upon it. On the fourth day, however, in came a case. He little knew that he was the first that I had ever had all to myself in my life. Perhaps he would not have looked quite so cheerful if he had realised it.

Poor chap, he had little enough to be cheery over either. He was an old soldier who had lost a good any teeth, but who had continued to find room between his nose and chin for a short black clay pipe. Lately there appeared a small sore on his nose which had spread, and become crusted. On feeling it I found it as hard as a streak of glue, with constant darting pains passing through it. Of course, there could be no question as to diagnosis. It was epitheliomatous cancer, caused by the irritation of the hot tobacco smoke. I sent him back to his village, and two days after I drove over in Cullingworth's dog-cart, and removed the growth. I only got a sovereign for it. But it may be a nucleus for cases. The old fellow did most admirably, and he has just been in (with a most aristocratic curl to his nostrils) to tell me that he has bought a box full of churchwardens. It was my first operation, and I daresay I was more nervous about it than my patient, but the result has given me confidence. I have fully made up my mind to let nothing pass me. Come what may, I am prepared to do it. Why should a man wait? Of course, I know that many men do; but surely one's nerve is more likely to be strong and one's knowledge fresh now than in twenty years.

Cases came dribbling in from day to day - all very poor people, and able to pay very poor fees - but still most welcome to me. The first week I took (including that operation fee) one pound seventeen and sixpence. The second, I got two pounds exactly. The third, I had two pounds five, and now I find that this last week has brought in two pounds eighteen; so I am moving in the right direction. Of course, it compares absurdly enough with Cullingworth's twenty pound a day, and my little quiet back-water seems a strange contrast to the noisy stream which pours for ever through his room. Still, I am quite satisfied, and I have no doubt at all that his original estimate of three hundred pounds for the first year will be amply justified. It would be a pleasant thing to think that if anything were really to happen at home, I should be able to be of some use to them. If things go on as they have begun, I shall soon have my feet firmly planted.

I was compelled, by the way, to forego an opening which a few months ago would have been the very summit of my ambition. You must know (possibly I told you), that immediately after I passed, I put my name down as a candidate for a surgeonship on the books of several of the big steamship lines. It was done as a forlorn hope, for a man has usually to wait several years before his turn comes round. Well, just a week after I started here, I got a telegram one night from Liverpool: "Join the Decia to-morrow as surgeon, not later than eight in the evening." It was from Staunton & Merivale, the famous South American firm, and the Decia is a fine 6000-ton passenger boat, doing the round journey by Bahia and Buenos Ayres to Rio and Valparaiso. I had a bad quarter of an hour, I can tell you. I don't think I was ever so undecided about anything in my life. Cullingworth was dead against my going, and his influence carried the day.

"My dear chap," said he, "you'd knock down the chief mate, and he'd spread you out with a handspike. You'd get tied by your thumbs to the rigging. You'd be fed on stinking water and putrid biscuits. I've been reading a novel about the merchant service, and I know."

When I laughed at his ideas of modern sea-going he tried another line.

"You're a bigger fool than I take you for if you go," said he. "Why, what can it lead to? All the money you earn goes to buy a blue coat, and daub it with lace. You think you're bound for Valparaiso, and you find yourself at the poor-house. You've got a rare opening here, and everything ready to your hand. You'll never get such another again."

And so it ended by my letting them have a wire to say that I could not come. It is strange when you come to a point where the road of your life obviously divides, and you take one turning or the other after vainly trying to be sure about the finger-post. I think after all I chose rightly. A ship's surgeon must remain a ship's surgeon, while here there is no horizon to my possibilities.

As to old Cullingworth, he is booming along as merrily as ever. You say in your last, that what you cannot understand is how he got his hold of the public in so short a time. That is just the point which I have found it hard to get light upon. He told me that after his first coming he had not a patient for a month, and that he was so disheartened that he very nearly made a moonlight exodus. At last, however, a few cases came his way - and he made such extraordinary cures of them, or else impressed them so by his eccentricity, that they would do nothing but talk of him. Some of his wonderful results got into the local press, though, after my Avonmouth experience, I should not like to guarantee that he did not himself convey them there. He showed me an almanac, which had a great circulation in the district.

It had an entry sandwiched in this way:

Aug. 15. Reform Bill passed 1867.

Aug. 16. Birth of Julius Caesar.

Aug. 17. Extraordinary cure by Dr. Cullingworth of a case of dropsy in Bradfield, 1881.

Aug. 18. Battle of Gravelotte, 1870.

It reads as if it were one of the landmarks of the latter half of the century. I asked him how on earth it got there; but I could only learn that the woman was fifty-six inches round the waist, and that he had treated her with elaterium.

That leads me to another point. You ask me whether his cures are really remarkable, and, if so, what his system is. I answer unhesitatingly, that his cures are very remarkable, indeed, and that I look upon him as a sort of Napoleon of medicine. His view is that the pharmacopaeal doses are in nearly every instance much too low. Excessive timidity has cut down the dose until it has ceased to produce a real effect upon the disease.

Medical men, according to his view, have been afraid of producing a poisonous effect with their drugs. With him, on the contrary, the whole art of medicine lies in judicious poisoning, and when the case is serious, his remedies are heroic. Where, in epilepsy, I should have given thirty-grain doses of bromide or chloral every four hours, he would give two drachms every three. No doubt it will seem to you very kill-or-cure, and I am myself afraid that a succession of coroners' inquests may check Cullingworth's career; but hitherto he has had no public scandal, while the cases which he has brought back to life have been numerous. He is the most fearless fellow. I have seen him pour opium into a dysenteric patient until my hair bristled. But either his knowledge or his luck always brings him out right.

Then there are other cures which depend, I think, upon his own personal magnetism. He is so robust and loud-voiced and hearty that a weak nervous patient goes away from him recharged with vitality. He is so perfectly confident that he can cure them, that he makes them perfectly confident that they can be cured; and you know how in nervous cases the mind reacts upon the body. If he chose to preserve crutches and sticks, as they do in the mediaeval churches, he might, I am sure, paper his consulting room with them. A favourite device of his with an impressionable patient is to name the exact hour of their cure. "My dear," he will say, swaying some girl about by the shoulders, with his nose about three inches from hers, "you'll feel better to-morrow at a quarter to ten, and at twenty past you'll be as well as ever you were in your life. Now, keep your eye on the clock, and see if I am not right." Next day, as likely as not, her mother will be in, weeping tears of joy; and another miracle has been added to Cullingworth's record. It may smell of quackery, but it is exceedingly useful to the patient.

Still I must confess that there is nothing about Cullingworth which jars me so much as the low view which he takes of our profession. I can never reconcile myself to his ideas, and yet I can never convert him to mine; so there will be a chasm there which sooner or later may open to divide us altogether. He will not acknowledge any philanthropic side to the question. A profession, in his view, is a means of earning a livelihood, and the doing good to our fellow mortals, is quite a secondary one.

"Why the devil should we do all the good, Munro?" he shouts. Eh, what? A butcher would do good to the race, would he not, if he served his chops out gratis through the window? He'd be a real benefactor; but he goes on selling them at a shilling the pound for all that. Take the case of a doctor who devotes himself to sanitary science. He flushes out drains, and keeps down infection. You call him a philanthropist! Well, I call him a traitor. That's it, Munro, a traitor and a renegade! Did you ever hear of a congress of lawyers for simplifying the law and discouraging litigation? What are the Medical Association and the General Council, and all these bodies for? Eh, laddie? For encouraging the best interests of the profession. Do you suppose they do that by making the population healthy? It's about time we had a mutiny among the general practitioners. If I had the use of half the funds which the Association has, I should spend part of them in drain-blocking, and the rest in the cultivation of disease germs, and the contamination of drinking water."

Of course, I told him that his views were diabolical; but, especially since that warning which I had from his wife, I discount everything that he says. He begins in earnest; but as he goes on the humour of exaggeration gets hold of him, and he winds up with things which he would never uphold in cold blood. However, the fact remains that we differ widely in our views of professional life, and I fear that we may come to grief over the question.

What do you think we have been doing lately? Building a stable - no less. Cullingworth wanted to have another one at the business place, as much, I think, for his patients as his horses; and, in his audacious way, he determined that he would build it himself. So at it we went, he, I, the coachman, Mrs. Cullingworth, and the coachman's wife. We dug foundations, got bricks in by the cartload, made our own mortar, and I think that we shall end by making a very fair job of it. It's not quite as flat-chested as we could wish; and I think that if I were a horse inside it, I should be careful about brushing against the walls; but still it will keep the wind and rain out when it is finished. Cullingworth talks of our building a new house for ourselves; but as we have three large ones already there does not seem to be any pressing need.

Talking about horses, we had no end of a fuss here the other day. Cullingworth got it into his head that he wanted a first-class riding horse; and as neither of the carriage ones would satisfy him, he commissioned a horse dealer to get him one. The man told us of a charger which one of the officers in the garrison was trying to get rid of. He did not conceal the fact that the reason why he wished to sell it was because he considered it to be dangerous; but, he added, that Captain Lucas had given L150 for it, and was prepared to sell it at seventy. This excited Cullingworth, and he ordered the creature to be saddled and brought round. It was a beautiful animal, coal black, with a magnificent neck and shoulders, but with a nasty backward tilt to its ears, and an unpleasant way of looking at you. The horse dealer said that our yard was too small to try the creature in; but Cullingworth clambered up upon its back and formally took possession of it by lamming it between the ears with the bone handle of his whip. Then ensued one of the most lively ten minutes that I can remember. The beast justified his reputation; but Cullingworth, although he was no horseman, stuck to him like a limpet. Backwards, forwards, sideways, on his fore feet, on his hind feet, with his back curved, with his back sunk, bucking and kicking, there was nothing the creature did not try. Cullingworth was sitting alternately on his mane and on the root of his tail - never by any chance in the saddle - he had lost both stirrups, and his knees were drawn up and his heels dug into the creature's ribs, while his hands clawed at mane, saddle, or ears, whichever he saw in front of him. He kept his whip, however; and whenever the brute eased down, Cullingworth lammed him once more with the bone handle. His idea, I suppose, was to break its spirit, but he had taken a larger contract than he could carry through. The animal bunched his four feet together, ducked down his head, arched his back like a yawning cat, and gave three convulsive springs into the air. At the first, Cullingworth's knees were above the saddle flaps, at the second his ankles were retaining a convulsive grip, at the third he flew forward like a stone out of a sling, narrowly missed the coping of the wall, broke with his head the iron bar which held some wire netting, and toppled back with a thud into the yard. Up he bounded with the blood streaming down his face, and running into our half-finished stables he seized a hatchet, and with a bellow of rage rushed at the horse. I caught him by the coat and put on a fourteen-stone drag, while the horse dealer (who was as white as a cheese) ran off with his horse into the street. Cullingworth broke away from my grip, and cursing incoherently, his face slobbered with blood, and his hatchet waving over his head, he rushed out of the yard - the most diabolical looking ruffian you can imagine. However, luckily for the dealer, he had got a good start, and Cullingworth was persuaded to come back and wash his face. We bound up his cut, and found him little the worse, except in his temper. But for me he would most certainly have paid seventy pounds for his insane outburst of rage against the animal.

I daresay you think it strange that I should write so much about this fellow and so little about anybody else; but the fact is, that I know nobody else, and that my whole circle is bounded by my patients, Cullingworth and his wife. They visit nobody, and nobody visits them. My living with them brings the same taboo from my brother doctors upon my head, although I have never done anything unprofessional myself. Who should I see in the street the other day but the McFarlanes, whom you will remember at Linlithgow? I was foolish enough to propose to Maimie McFarlane once, and she was sensible enough to refuse me. What I should have done had she accepted me, I can't imagine; for that was three years ago, and I have more ties and less prospect of marriage now than then. Well, there's no use yearning for what you can't have, and there's no other man living to whom I would speak about the matter at all; but life is a deadly, lonely thing when a man has no one on his side but himself. Why is it that I am sitting here in the moonlight writing to you, except that I am craving for sympathy and fellowship? I get it from you, too - as much as one friend ever got from another - and yet there are some sides to my nature with which neither wife nor friend nor any one else can share. If you cut your own path, you must expect to find yourself alone upon it.

Heigh ho! it's nearly dawn, and I as wakeful as ever. It is chilly, and I have draped a blanket round me. I've heard that this is the favourite hour of the suicide, and I see that I've been tailing off in the direction of melancholy myself. Let me wind up on a lighter chord by quoting Cullingworth's latest article. I must tell you that he is still inflamed by the idea of his own paper, and his brain is in full eruption, sending out a perpetual stream of libellous paragraphs, doggerel poems, social skits, parodies, and articles. He brings them all to me, and my table is already piled with them. Here is his latest, brought up to my room after he had undressed. It was the outcome of some remarks I had made about the difficulty which our far-off descendants may have in determining what the meaning is of some of the commonest objects of our civilisation, and as a corollary how careful we should be before we become dogmatic about the old Romans or Egyptians.

"At the third annual meeting of the New Guinea Archaeological Society a paper was read upon recent researches on the supposed site of London, together with some observations upon hollow cylinders in use among the ancient Londoners. Several examples of these metallic cylinders or tubings were on exhibition in the hall, and were passed round for inspection among the audience. The learned lecturer prefaced his remarks by observing that on account of the enormous interval of time which separated them from the days when London was a flourishing city, it behoved them to be very guarded in any conclusions to which they might come as to the habits of the inhabitants. Recent research appeared to have satisfactorily established the fact that the date of the final fall of London was somewhat later than that of the erection of the Egyptian Pyramids. A large building had recently been unearthed near the dried-up bed of the river Thames; and there could be no question from existing records that this was the seat of the law-making council among the ancient Britons - or Anglicans, as they were sometimes called. The lecturer proceeded to point out that the bed of the Thames had been tunnelled under by a monarch named Brunel, who is supposed by some authorities to have succeeded Alfred the Great. The open spaces of London, he went on to remark, must have been far from safe, as the bones of lions, tigers, and other extinct forms of carnivora had been discovered in the Regent's Park. Having briefly refferred to the mysterious structures known as `pillar-boxes,' which are scattered thickly over the city, and which are either religious in their origin, or else may be taken as marking the tombs of Anglican chiefs, the lecturer passed on to the cylindrical piping. This had been explained by the Patagonian school as being a universal system of lightning-conductors. He (the lecturer) could not assent to this theory. In a series of observations, extending over several months, he had discovered the important fact that these lines of tubing, if followed out, invariably led to large hollow metallic reservoirs which were connected with furnaces. No one who knew how addicted the ancient Britons were to the use of tobacco could doubt what this meant. Evidently large quantities of the herb were burned in the central chamber, and the aromatic and narcotic vapour was carried through the tubes to the house of every citizen, so that he might inhale it at will. Having illustrated his remarks by a series of diagrams, the lecturer concluded by saying that, although true

Sir A. C. Doyle

science was invariably cautious and undogmatic, it was none the less an incontestable fact that so much light had been thrown upon old London, that every action of the citizens' daily life was known, from the taking of a tub in the morning, until after a draught of porter he painted himself blue before retiring to rest."

After all, I daresay this explanation of the London gas pipes is not more absurd than some of our shots about the Pyramids, or ideas of life among the Babylonians.

Well, good-bye, old chap; this is a stupid inconsequential letter, but life has been more quiet and less interesting just of late. I may have something a little more moving for my next.

IX.

1 THE PARADE, BRADFIELD,
23rd April, 1882.

I have some recollection, my dear Bertie, that when I wrote you a rambling disconnected sort of letter about three weeks ago, I wound up by saying that I might have something more interesting to tell you next time. Well, so it has turned out! The whole game is up here, and I am off upon a fresh line of rails altogether. Cullingworth is to go one way and I another; and yet I am glad to say that there has not been any quarrel between us. As usual, I have begun my letter at the end, but I'll work up to it more deliberately now, and let you know exactly how it came about.

And first of all, a thousand thanks for your two long letters, which lie before me as I write. There is little enough personal news in them, but I can quite understand that the quiet happy routine of your life reels off very smoothly from week to week. On the other hand, you give me plenty of proof of that inner life which is to me so very much more interesting. After all, we may very well agree to differ. You think some things are proved which I don't believe in. You think some things edifying which do not appear to me to be so. Well, I know that you are perfectly honest in your belief. I am sure you give me credit for being the same. The future wilt decide which of us is right. The survival of the truest is a constant law, I fancy, though it must be acknowledged that it is very slow in action. You make a mistake, however, in assuming that those who think as I do are such a miserable minority. The whole essence of our thought is independence and individual judgment; so that we don't get welded into single bodies as the churches do, and have no opportunity of testing our own strength. There are, no doubt, all shades of opinion among us; but if you merely include those who in their private hearts disbelieve the doctrines usually accepted, and think that sectarian churches tend to evil rather than good, I fancy that the figures would be rather surprising. When I read your letter, I made a list of all those men with whom I ever had intimate talk upon such matters. I got seventeen names, with four orthodox. Cullingworth tried and got twelve names, with one orthodox. From all sides, one hears that every church complains of the absence of men in the congregations. The women predominate three to one. Is it that women are more earnest than men? I think it is quite the other way. But the men are following their reason, and the women their emotion. It is the women only who keep orthodoxy alive.

No, you mustn't be too sure of that majority of yours. Taking the scientific, the medical, the professional classes, I question whether it exists at all. The clergy, busy in their own limited circles, and coming in contact only with those who agree with them, have not realised how largely the rising generation has out-grown them. And (with exceptions like yourself) it is not the most lax, but the BEST of the younger men, the larger-brained and the larger-hearted, who have shaken themselves most clear of the old theology. They cannot abide its want of charity, it's limitations of

God's favours, its claims for a special Providence, its dogmatism about what seems to be false, its conflict with what we know to be true. We KNOW that man has ascended, not descended; so what is the value of a scheme of thought which depends upon the supposition of his fall? We KNOW that the world was not made in six days, that the sun could never be stopped since it was never moving, and that no man ever lived three days in a fish; so what becomes of the inspiration of a book which contains such statements? "Truth, though it crush me!"

There, now, you see what comes of waving the red rag! Let me make a concession to appease you. I do believe that Christianity in its different forms has been the very best thing for the world during all this long barbarous epoch. Of course, it has been the best thing, else Providence would not have permitted it. The engi-engineer knows best what tools to use in strengthening his own machine. But when you say that this is the best and last tool which will be used, you are laying down the law a little too much.

Now, first of all, I want to tell you about how the practice has been going on. The week after I wrote last showed a slight relapse. I only took two pounds. But on the next I took a sudden jump up to three pounds seven shillings, and this last week I took three pounds ten. So it was steadily creeping up; and I really thought that I saw my road clear in front of me, when the bolt suddenly fell from the blue. There were reasons, however, which prevented my being very disappointed when it did come down; and these I must make clear to you.

I think that I mentioned, when I gave you a short

sketch of my dear old mother, that she has a very high standard of family honour. She really tries to live up to the Percy-Plantagenet blend which is said to flow in our veins; and it is only our empty pockets which prevent her from sailing through life, like the grande dame that she is, throwing largesse to right and left, with her head in the air and her soul in the clouds. I have often heard her say (and I am quite convinced that she meant it) that she would far rather see any one of us in our graves than know that we had committed a dishonourable action. Yes; for all her softness and femininity, she could freeze iron-hard at the suspicion of baseness; and I have seen the blood flush from her white cap to her lace collar when she has heard of an act of meanness.

Well, she had heard some details about the Cullingworths which displeased her when I first knew them. Then came the smash-up at Avonmouth, and my mother liked them less and less. She was averse to my joining them in Bradfield, and it was only by my sudden movement at the end that I escaped a regular prohibition. When I got there, the very first question she asked (when I told her of their prosperity) was whether they had paid their Avonmouth creditors. I was compelled to answer that they had not. In reply she wrote imploring me to come away, and saying that, poor as our family was, none of them had ever fallen so low as to enter into a business partnership with a man of unscrupulous character and doubtful antecedents. I answered that Cullingworth spoke sometimes of paying his creditors, that Mrs. Cullingworth was in favour of it also, and that it seemed to me to be unreasonable to expect that I should sacrifice a good opening on account of things with which I had no connection. I assured her that if Cullingworth did anything from then onwards which seemed to me dishonourable, I would disassociate myself from him, and I mentioned that I had already refused to adopt some of his professional methods. Well, in reply to this, my mother wrote a pretty violent letter about what she thought of Cullingworth, which led to another from me defending him, and showing that there were some deep and noble traits in his character. That produced another still more outspoken letter from her; and so the correspondence went on, she attacking and I defending, until a serious breach seemed to be opening between us. I refrained from writing at last, not out of ill temper, but because I thought that if she were given time she would cool down, and take, perhaps, a more reasonable view of the situation. My father, from the short note which he sent me, seemed to think the whole business absolutely irregular, and to refuse to believe my accounts of Cullingworth's practice and receipts. This double opposition, from the very people whose interests had really been nearest my heart in the whole affair, caused me to be less disappointed than I should otherwise have been when it all came to an end. In fact, I was quite in the humour to finish it myself when Fate did it for me.

Now about the Cullingworths. Madam is as amiable as ever; and yet somehow, unless I am deceiving myself, she has changed somewhat of late in her feelings towards me. I have turned upon her suddenly more than once, and caught the skirt of a glance which was little less than malignant. In one or two small matters I have also detected a hardness in her which I had never observed before. Is it that I have intruded too much into their family life? Have I come between the husband and the wife? Goodness knows I have striven with all my little stock of tact to avoid doing so. And yet I have often felt that my position was a false one. Perhaps a young man attaches too much importance to a woman's glances and gestures. He wishes to assign a definite meaning to each, when they may be only the passing caprice of the moment. Ah, well, I have nothing to blame myself with; and in any case it will soon be all over now.

And then I have seen something of the same sort in Cullingworth; but he is so strange a being that I never attach much importance to his variations. He glares at me like an angry bull occasionally; and then when I ask him what is the matter, he growls out, "Oh, nothing!" and turns on his heel. Then at other times he is so cordial and friendly that he almost overdoes it, and I find myself wondering whether he is not acting. It must seem ungracious to you that I should speak so of a man who has been my benefactor; and it seems so to me also, but still that IS the impression which he leaves upon me sometimes. It's an absurd idea, too; for what possible object could his wife and he have in pretending to be amiable, if they did not really feel so? And yet you know the feeling that you get when a man smiles with his lips and not with his eyes.

One day we went to the Central Hotel billiard-room in the evening to play a match. Our form is just about the same, and we should have bad an enjoyable game if it had not been for that queer temper of his. He had been in a sullen humour the whole day, pretending not to hear what I said to him, or else giving snappy answers, and looking like a thunder-cloud. I was determined not to have a row, so I took no notice at all of his continual provocations, which, instead of pacifying him, seemed to encourage him to become more offensive. At the end of the match, wanting two to win, I put down the white which was in the jaws of the pocket. He cried out that this was bad form. I contended that it was folly to refrain from doing it when one was only two off game, and, on his continuing to make remarks, I appealed to the marker, who took the same view as I did. This opposition only increased his anger, and he suddenly broke out into most violent language, abusing me in unmeasured terms. I said to him, "If you have anything to say to me, Cullingworth, come out into the street and say it there. It's a caddish thing to speak like that before the marker." He lifted his cue, and I thought he was going to strike me with it; but he flung it clattering on the floor, and chucked half a crown to the man. When we got out in the street, he began at once in as offensive a tone as ever.

"That's enough, Cullingworth," I said. "I've stood already rather more than I can carry."

We were in the bright light of a shop window at that moment. He looked at me, and looked a second time, uncertain what to do. At any moment I might have found myself in a desperate street row with a man who was my medical partner. I gave no provocation, but kept myself keenly on the alert. Suddenly, to my relief, he burst out laughing (such a roar as made the people stop on the other side of the road), and passing his arm through mine, he hurried me down the street.

"Devil of a temper you've got, Munro," said he. "By Crums, it's hardly safe to go out with you. I never know what you're going to do next. Eh, what? You mustn't be peppery with me, though; for I mean well towards you, as you'll see before you get finished with me."

I have told you this trivial little scene, Bertie, to show the strange way in which Cullingworth springs quarrels upon me; suddenly, without the slightest possible provocation, taking a most offensive tone, and then when he sees he has goaded me to the edge of my endurance, turning the whole thing to chaff. This has occurred again and again recently; and, when coupled with the change in Mrs. Cullingworth's demeanour, makes one feel that something has happened to change one's relations. What that something may be, I give you my word that I have no more idea than you have. Between their coldness, however, and my unpleasant correspondence with my mother, I was often very sorry that I had not taken the South American liner.

Cullingworth is preparing for the issue of our new paper. He has carried the matter through with his usual energy, but he doesn't know enough about local affairs to be able to write about them, and it is a question whether he can interest the people here in anything else. At present we are prepared to run the paper single-handed; we are working seven hours a day at the practice; we are building a stable; and in our odd hours we are practising at our magnetic ship-protector, with which Cullingworth is still well pleased, though he wants to get it more perfect before submitting it to the Admiralty.

His mind runs rather on naval architecture at present, and he has been devising an ingenious method of preventing wooden-sided vessels from being crippled by artillery fire. I did not think much of his magnetic attractor, because it seemed to me that even if it had all the success that he claimed for it, it would merely have the effect of substituting some other metal for steel in the manufacture of shells. This new project has, however, more to recommend it. This is the idea, as put in his own words; and, as he has been speaking of little else for the last two days, I ought to remember them.

"If you've got your armour there, laddie, it will be pierced," says he. "Put up forty feet thick of steel; and I'll build a gun that will knock it into tooth-powder. It would blow away, and set the folk coughing after I had one shot at it. But you can't pierce armour which only drops after the shot has passed through. What's the good of it? Why it keeps out the water. That's the main thing, after all. I call it the Cullingworth spring-shutter screen. Eh, what, Munro? I wouldn't take a quarter of a million for the idea. You see how it would work. Spring shutters are furled all along the top of the bulwarks where the hammocks used to be. They are in sections, three feet broad, we will say, and capable when let down of reaching the keel. Very well! Enemy sends a shot through Section A of the side. Section A shutter is lowered. Only a thin film, you see, but enough to form a temporary plug. Enemy's ram knocks in sections B, C, D of the side. What do you do? Founder? Not a bit; you lower sections B, C, and D of Cullingworth's spring-shutter screen. Or you knock a hole on a rock. The same thing again. It's a ludicrous sight to see a big ship founder when so simple a precaution would absolutely save her. And it's equally good for ironclads also. A shot often starts their plates and admits water without breaking them. Down go your shutters, and all is well."

That's his idea, and he is busy on a model made out of the steels of his wife's stays. It sounds plausible, but he has the knack of making anything plausible when he is allowed to slap his hands and bellow.

We are both writing novels, but I fear that the results don't bear out his theory that a man may do anything which he sets his will to. I thought mine was not so bad (I have done nine chapters), but Cullingworth says he has read it all before, and that it is much too conventional. We must rivet the attention of the public from the start, he says. Certainly, his own is calculated to do so, for it seems to me to be wild rubbish. The end of his first chapter is the only tolerable point that he has made. A fraudulent old baronet is running race-horses on the cross. His son, who is just coming of age, is an innocent youth. The news of the great race of the year has just been received.

"Sir Robert tottered into the room with dry lips and a ghastly face.

"`My poor boy!' he cried. `Prepare for the worst!'

"`Our horse has lost!' cried the young heir, springing from his chair.

"The old man threw himself in agony upon the rug. `No, no!' he screamed. `IT HAS WON!'"

Most of it, however, is poor stuff, and we are each agreed that the other was never meant for a novelist.

So much for our domestic proceedings, and all these little details which you say you like to hear of. Now I must tell you of the great big change in my affairs, and how it came about.

I have told you about the strange, sulky behaviour of Cullingworth, which has been deepening from day to day. Well, it seemed to reach a climax this morning, and on our way to the rooms I could hardly get a word out of him. The place was fairly crowded with patients, but my own share was rather below the average. When I had finished I added a chapter to my novel, and waited until he and his wife were ready for the daily bag-carrying homewards.

It was half-past three before he had done. I heard him stamp out into the passage, and a moment later he came banging into my room. I saw in an instant that some sort of a crisis had come.

"Munro," he cried, "this practice is going to the devil!"

"Ah!" said I. "How's that?

"It's going to little pieces, Munro. I've been taking figures, and I know what I am talking about. A month ago I was seeing six hundred a week. Then I dropped to five hundred and eighty; then to five-seventy-five; and now to five-sixty. What do you think of that?"

"To be honest, I don't think much of it," I answered. "The summer is coming on. You are losing all your coughs and colds and sore throats. Every practice must dwindle at this time of year."

"That's all very well," said he, pacing up and down the room, with his hands thrust into his pockets, and his great shaggy eyebrows knotted together. "You may put it down to that, but I think quite differently about it."

"What do you put it down to, then?"

"To you."

"How's that?" I asked.

"Well," said he, "you must allow that it is a very queer coincidence - if it is a coincidence - that from the day when your plate was put up my practice has taken a turn for the worse."

"I should be very sorry to think it was cause and effect," I answered. "How do you think that my presence could have hurt you?"

"I'll tell you frankly, old chap," said he, putting on suddenly that sort of forced smile which always seems to me to have a touch of a sneer in it. "You see, many of my patients are simple country folk, half imbecile for the most part, but then the half-crown of an imbecile is as good as any other half-crown. They come to my door, and they see two names, and their silly jaws begin to drop, and they say to each other, `There's two of 'em here. It's Dr. Cullingworth we want to see, but if we go in we'll be shown as likely as not to Dr. Munro.' So it ends in some cases in their not coming at all. Then there are the women. Women don't care a toss whether you are a Solomon, or whether you are hot from an asylum. It's all personal with them. You fetch them, or you don't fetch them. I know how to work them, but they won't come if they think they are going to be turned over to anybody else. That's what I put the falling away down to."

"Well," said I, "that's easily set right." I marched out of the room and downstairs, with both Cullingworth and his wife behind me. Into the yard I went, and, picking up a big hammer, I started for the front door, with the pair still at my heels. I got the forked end of the hammer under my plate, and with a good wrench I brought the whole thing clattering on to the pavement.

"That won't interfere with you any more," said I.

"What do you intend to do now?" he asked.

"Oh, I shall find plenty to do. Don't you worry about that," I answered.

"Oh, but this is all rot," said he, picking up the plate. "Come along upstairs and let us see where we stand."

We filed off once more, he leading with the huge brass "Dr. Munro" under his arm; then the little woman, and then this rather perturbed and bemuddled young man. He and his wife sat on the deal table in the consulting room, like a hawk and a turtle-dove on the same perch, while I leaned against the mantelpiece with my hands in my pockets. Nothing could be more prosaic and informal; but I knew very well that I was at a crisis of my life. Before, it was only a choosing between two roads. Now my main track had run suddenly to nothing, and I must go back or find a bye-path.

"It's this way, Cullingworth," said I. "I am very much obliged to you, and to you, Mrs. Cullingworth, for all your kindness and good wishes, but I did not come here to spoil your practice; and, after what you have told me, it is quite impossible for me to work with you any more."

"Well, my boy," said he, "I am inclined myself to think that we should do better apart; and that's Hetty's idea also, only she is too polite to say so."

"It is a time for plain speaking," I answered, it and we

may as well thoroughly understand each other. If I have done your practice any harm, I assure you that I am heartily sorry, and I shall do all I can to repair it. I cannot say more."

"What are you going to do, then?" asked Cullingworth.

"I shall either go to sea or else start a practice on my own account."

"But you have no money."

"Neither had you when you started."

"Ah, that was different. Still, it may be that you are right. You'll find it a stiff pull at first."

"Oh, I am quite prepared for that."

"Well, you know, Munro, I feel that I am responsible to you to some extent, since I persuaded you not to take that ship the other day."

"It was a pity, but it can't be helped."

"We must do what we can to make up. Now, I tell you what I am prepared to do. I was talking about it with Hetty this morning, and she thought as I did. If we were to allow you one pound a week until you got your legs under you, it would encourage you to start for yourself, and you could pay it back as soon as you were able."

"It is very kind of you," said I. "If you would let the matter stand just now, I should like just to take a short walk by myself, and to think it all over."

So the Cullingworths did their bag-procession through the doctors' quarter alone to-day, and I walked to the park, where I sat down on one of the seats, lit a cigar, and thought the whole matter over. I was down on my luck at first; but the balmy air and the smell of spring and the budding flowers soon set me right again. I began my last letter among the stars, and I am inclined to finish this one among the flowers, for they are rare companions when one's mind is troubled. Most things on this earth, from a woman's beauty to the taste of a nectarine, seem to be the various baits with which Nature lures her silly gudgeons. They shall eat, they shall propagate, and for the sake of pleasing them-selves they shall hurry down the road which has been laid out for them. But there lurks no bribe in the smell and beauty of the flower. It's charm has no ulterior motive.

Well, I sat down there and brooded. In my heart I did not believe that Cullingworth had taken alarm at so trifling a decrease. That could not have been his real reason for driving me from the practice. He had found me in the way in his domestic life, no doubt, and he had devised this excuse for getting rid of me. Whatever the reason was, it was sufficiently plain that all my hopes of building up a surgical practice, which should keep parallel with his medical one, were for ever at an end. On the whole, bearing in mind my mother's opposition, and the continual janglings which we had had during the last few weeks, I was not very sorry. On the contrary, a sudden curious little thrill of happiness took me somewhere about the back of the midriff, and, as a drift of rooks passed cawing over my head, I began cawing also in the overflow of my spirits.

And then as I walked back I considered how far I could

avail myself of this money from Cullingworth. It was not much, but it would be madness to start without it, for I had sent home the little which I had saved at Horton's. I had not more than six pounds in the whole world. I reflected that the money could make no difference to Cullingworth, with his large income, while it made a vast one to me. I should repay him in a year or two at the latest. Perhaps I might get on so well as to be able to dispense with it almost at once. There could be no doubt that it was the representations of Cullingworth as to my future prospects in Bradfield which had made me refuse the excellent appointment in the Decia. I need not therefore have any scruples at accepting some temporary assistance from his hands. On my return, I told him that I had decided to do so, and thanked him at the same time for his generosity.

"That's all right," said he. "Hetty, my dear, get a bottle of fez in, and we shall drink success to Munro's new venture."

It seemed only the other day that he had been drinking my entrance into partnership; and here we were, the same three, sipping good luck to my exit from it! I'm afraid our second ceremony was on both sides the heartier of the two.

"I must decide now where I am to start," I remarked. "What I want is some nice little town where all the people are rich and ill."

"I suppose you wouldn't care to settle here in Bradfield?" asked Cullingworth.

"Well, I cannot see much point in that. If I harmed you as a partner, I might do so more as a rival. If I succeeded it might be at your expense."

"Well," said he, "choose your town, and my offer still holds good."

We hunted out an atlas, and laid the map of England before us on the table. Cities and villages lay beneath me as thick as freckles, and yet there was nothing to lead me to choose one rather than another.

"I think it should be some place large enough to give you plenty of room for expansion," said he.

"Not too near London," added Mrs. Cullingworth.

"And, above all, a place where I know nobody," said I. "I can rough it by myself, but I can't keep up appearances before visitors."

"What do you say to Stockwell?" said Cullingworth, putting the amber of his pipe upon a town within thirty miles of Bradfield.

I had hardly heard of the place, but I raised my glass. "Well, here's to Stockwell!" I cried; "I shall go there to-morrow morning and prospect." We all drank the toast (as you will do at Lowell when you read this); and so it is arranged, and you may rely upon it that I shall give you a full and particular account of the result.

X.

1 CADOGAN TERRACE, BIRCHESPOOL, i
21st May, 1882.

My dear old chap, things have been happening, and I must tell you all about it. Sympathy is a strange thing; for though I never see you, the mere fact that you over there in New England are keenly interested in what I am doing and thinking, makes my own life in old England very much more interesting to me. The thought of you is like a good staff in my right hand.

The unexpected has happened so continually in my life that it has ceased to deserve the name. You remember that in my last I had received my dismissal, and was on the eve of starting for the little country town of Stockwell to see if there were any sign of a possible practice there. Well, in the morning, before I came down to breakfast, I was putting one or two things into a bag, when there came a timid knock at my door, and there was Mrs. Cullingworth in her dressing-jacket, with her hair down her back.

"Would you mind coming down and seeing James, Dr. Munro?" said she. "He has been very strange all night, and I am afraid that he is ill."

Down I went, and found Cullingworth looking rather red in the face, and a trifle wild about the eyes. He was sitting up in bed, with the neck of his nightgown open, and an acute angle of hairy chest exposed. He had a sheet of paper, a pencil, and a clinical thermometer upon the coverlet in front of him.

"Deuced interesting thing, Munro," said he. "Come and look at this temperature chart. I've been taking it every quarter of an hour since I couldn't sleep, and it's up and down till it looks like the mountains in the geography books. We'll have some drugs in - eh, what, Munro? - and by Crums, we'll revolutionise all their ideas about fevers. I'll write a pamphlet from personal experiment that will make all their books clean out of date, and they'll have to tear them up and wrap sandwiches in them."

He was talking in the rapid slurring way of a man who has trouble coming. I looked at his chart, and saw that he was over 102 degrees. His pulse rub-a-dubbed under my fingers, and his skin sent a glow into my hand.

"Any symptoms?" I asked, sitting down on the side of his bed.

"Tongue like a nutmeg-grater," said he, thrusting it out. "Frontal headache, renal pains, no appetite, and a mouse nibbling inside my left elbow. That's as far as we've got at present."

"I'll tell you what it is, Cullingworth," said I. "You have a touch of rheumatic fever, and you will have to lie by for a bit."

"Lie by be hanged!" he cried. "I've got a hundred people to see to-day. My boy, I must be down there if I have the rattle in my throat. I didn't build up a practice to have it ruined by a few ounces of lactic acid."

"James dear, you can easily build up another one," said his wife, in her cooing voice. "You must do what Dr. Munro tells you."

"Well," said I, "you'll want looking after, and your practice will want looking after, and I am quite ready to do both. But I won't take the responsibility unless you give me your word that you will do what you are told."

"If I'm to have any doctoring it must come from you, laddie," he said; "for if I was to turn my toes up in the public square, there's not a man here who would do more than sign my certificate. By Crums, they might get the salts and oxalic acid mixed up if they came to treat me, for there's no love lost between us. But I want to go down to the practice all the same."

"It's out of the question. You know the sequel of this complaint. You'll have endocarditis, embolism, thrombosis, metastatic abscesses - you know the danger as well as I do."

He sank back into his bed laughing.

"I take my complaints one at a time, thank you," said he. "I wouldn't be so greedy as to have all those - eh, Munro, what? - when many another poor devil hasn't got an ache to his back." The four posts of his bed quivered with his laughter. "Do what you like, laddie - but I say, mind, if anything should happen, no tomfoolery over my grave. If you put so much as a stone there, by Crums, Munro, I'll come back in the dead of the night and plant it on the pit of your stomach."

Nearly three weeks passed before he could set his foot to the ground again. He wasn't such a bad patient, after all; but he rather complicated my treatment by getting in all sorts of phials and powders, and trying experiments upon his own symptoms. It was impossible to keep him quiet, and our only means of retaining him in bed was to allow him all the work that he could do there.

He wrote copiously, built up models of his patent screen, and banged off pistols at his magnetic target, which he had rigged tip on the mantelpiece. Nature has given him a constitution of steel, however, and he hook off his malady more quickly and more thoroughly than the most docile of sufferers.

In the meantime, Mrs. Cullingworth and I ran the practice together. As a substitute for him I was a dreadful failure. They would not believe in me in the least. I felt that I was as flat as water after champagne. I could not address them from the stairs, nor push them about, nor prophesy to the anaeemic women. I was much too solemn and demure after what they had been accustomed to. However, I held the thing together as best I could, and I don't think that he found the practice much the worse when he was able to take it over. I could not descend to what I thought was unprofessional, but I did my very best to keep the wheels turning.

Well, I know that I am a shocking bad story-teller, but I just try to get things as near the truth as I can manage it. If I only knew how to colour it up, I could make some of this better reading. I can get along when I am on one line, but it is when I have to bring in a second line of events that I understand what C. means when he says that I will never be able to keep myself in nibs by what I earn in literature.

The second line is this, that I had written to my mother on the same night that I wrote to you last, telling her that there need no longer be a shadow of a disagreement between us, because everything was arranged, and I was going to leave Cullingworth at once. Then within a couple of posts I had to write again and announce that my departure was indefinitely postponed, and that I was actually doing his whole practice. Well, the dear old lady was very angry. I don't suppose she quite understood how temporary the necessity was, and how impossible it would have been to leave Cullingworth in the lurch. She was silent for nearly three weeks, and then she wrote a very stinging letter (and she handles her adjectives most deftly when she likes). She went so far as to say that Cullingworth was a "bankrupt swindler," and that I had dragged the family honour in the dirt by my prolonged association with him. This letter came on the morning of the very last day that my patient was confined to the house. When I returned from work I found him sitting in his dressing-gown downstairs. His wife, who had driven home, was beside him. To my surprise, when I congratulated him on being fit for work again, his manner (which had been most genial during his illness) was as ungracious as before our last explanation. His wife, too, seemed to avoid my eye, and cocked her chin at me when she spoke.

"Yes, I'll take it over to-morrow," said he. "What do I owe you for looking after it?"

"Oh, it was all in the day's work," said I.

"Thank you, I had rather have strict business," he answered. "You know where you are then, but a favour is a thing with no end to it. What d'you put it at?"

"I never thought about it in that light."

"Well, think about it now. A locum would have cost me four guineas a week. Four fours sixteen. Make it twenty. Well, I promised to allow you a pound a week, and you were to pay it back. I'll put twenty pounds to your credit account, and you'll have it every week as sure as Saturday."

"Thank you," said I. "If you are so anxious to make a business matter of it, you can arrange it so." I could not make out, and cannot make out now, what had happened to freeze them up so; but I supposed that they had been talking it over, and came to the conclusion that I was settling down too much upon the old lines, and that they must remind me that I was under orders to quit. They might have done it with more tact.

To cut a long story short, on the very day that Cullingworth was able to resume his work I started off for Stockwell, taking with me only a bag, for it was merely a prospecting expedition, and I intended to return for my luggage if I saw reason for hope. Alas! there was not the faintest. The sight of the place would have damped the most sanguine man that ever lived. It is one of those picturesque little English towns with a history and little else. A Roman trench and a Norman keep are its principal products. But to me the most amazing thing about it was the cloud of doctors which had settled upon it. A double row of brass plates flanked the principal street. Where their patients came from I could not imagine, unless they practised upon each other. The host of the "Bull" where I had my modest lunch explained the mystery to some extent by saying that, as there was pure country with hardly a hamlet for nearly twelve miles in every direction, it was in these scattered farm-houses that the Stockwell doctors found their patients. As I chatted with him a middle-aged, dusty-booted man trudged up the street. "There's Dr. Adam," said he. "He's only a new-comer, but they say that some o' these days he'll be starting his carriage." "What do you mean by a new-comer?" I asked. "Oh, he's scarcely been here ten years," said the landlord. "Thank you," said I. "Can you tell me when the next train leaves for Bradfield?" So back I came, rather heavy at heart, and having spent ten or twelve shillings which I could ill afford. My fruitless journey seemed a small thing, however, when I thought of the rising Stockwellite with his ten years and his dusty boots. I can trudge along a path, however rough, if it will but lead to something; but may kindly Fate keep me out of all cul-de-sacs!

The Cullingworths did not receive me cordially upon my return. There was a singular look upon both their faces which seemed to ME to mean that they were disappointed at this hitch in getting rid of me. When I think of their absolute geniality a few days ago, and their markedly reserved manner now, I can make no sense out of it. I asked Cullingworth point blank what it meant, but he only turned it off with a forced laugh, and some nonsense about my thin skin. I think that I am the last man in the world to take offence where none is meant; but at any rate I determined to end the matter by leaving Bradfield at once. It had struck me, during my journey back from Stockwell, that Birchespool would be a good place; so on the very next day I started off, taking my luggage with me, and bidding a final good-bye to Cullingworth and his wife.

"You rely upon me, laddie," said C. with something of his old geniality, as we shook hands on parting. "You get a good house in a central position, put up your plate and hold on by your toe-nails. Charge little or nothing until you get a connection, and none of your professional haw-dammy or you are a broken man. I'll see that you don't stop steaming for want of coal."

So with that comforting assurance I left them on the platform of the Bradfield station. The words seem kind, do they not? and yet taking this money jars every nerve in my body. When I find that I can live on bread and water without it, I will have no more of it. But to do without it now would be for the man who cannot swim to throw off his life-belt.

I had plenty of time on my way to Birchespool to reflect upon my prospects and present situation. My baggage consisted of a large brassplate, a small leather trunk, and a hat-box. The plate with my name engraved upon it was balanced upon the rack above my head. In my box were a stethoscope, several medical books, a second pair of boots, two suits of clothes, my linen and my toilet things. With this, and the five pounds eighteen shillings which remain in my purse, I was sallying out to clear standing-room, and win the right to live from my fellow-men. But at least there was some chance of permanency about this; and if there was the promise of poverty and hardship, there was also that of freedom. I should have no Lady Saltire to toss up her chin because I had my own view of things, no Cullingworth to fly out at me about nothing. I would be my own - my very own. I capered up and down the carriage at the thought. After all, I had everything to gain and nothing in the whole wide world to lose. And I had youth and strength and energy, and the whole science of medicine packed in between my two ears. I felt as exultant as though I were going to take over some practice which lay ready for me.

It was about four in the afternoon when I reached Birchespool, which is fifty-three miles by rail from Bradfield. It may be merely a name to you, and, indeed, until I set foot in it I knew nothing of it myself; but I can tell you now that it has a population of a hundred and thirty thousand souls (about the same as Bradfield), that it is mildly manufacturing, that it is within an hour's journey of the sea, that it has an aristocratic western suburb with a mineral well, and that the country round is exceedingly beautiful. It is small enough to have a character of its own, and large enough for solitude, which is always the great charm of a city, after the offensive publicity of the country.

When I turned out with my brass plate, my trunk, and my hat-box upon the Birchespool platform, I sat down and wondered what my first move should be. Every penny was going to be of the most vital importance to me, and I must plan things within the compass of that tiny purse. As I sat pondering, there came a sight of interest, for I heard a burst of cheering with the blare of a band upon the other side of the station, and then the pioneers and leading files of a regiment came swinging on to the platform. They wore white sun-hats, and were leaving for Malta, in anticipation of war in Egypt. They were young soldiers - English by the white facings - with a colonel whose moustache reached his shoulders, and a number of fresh-faced long-legged subalterns. I chiefly remember one of the colour-sergeants, a man of immense size and ferocious face, who leaned upon his Martini, with two little white kittens peeping over either shoulder from the flaps of his knapsack. I was so moved at the sight of these youngsters going out to do their best for the dear old country, that I sprang up on my box, took off my hat, and gave them three cheers. At first the folk on my side looked at me in their bovine fashion - like a row of cows over a wall. At the second a good many joined, and at the third my own voice was entirely lost. So I turned to go my way, and the soldier laddies to go theirs; and I wondered which of us had the stiffest and longest fight before us.

I left my baggage at the office, and jumped into a tramcar which was passing the station, with the intention of looking for lodgings, as I judged that they would be cheaper than an hotel. The conductor interested himself in my wants in that personal way which makes me think that the poorer classes in England are one of the kindliest races on earth. Policemen, postmen, railway guards, busmen, what good helpful fellows they all are! This one reckoned the whole thing out, how this street was central but dear, and the other was out-of-the-way but cheap, and finally dropped me at a medium shabby-genteel kind of thoroughfare called Cadogan Terrace, with instructions that I was to go down there and see how I liked it.

I could not complain of a limited selection, for a "to let " or "apartments" was peeping out of every second window. I went into the first attractive house that I saw, and interviewed the rather obtuse and grasping old lady who owned it. A sitting-bed-room was to be had for thirteen shillings a week. As I had never hired rooms before, I had no idea whether this was cheap or dear; but I conclude it was the latter, since on my raising my eyebrows as an experiment she instantly came down to tenshillings and sixpence. I tried another look and an exclamation of astonishment; but as she stood firm, I gathered that I had touched the bottom.

"Your rooms are quite clean?" I asked, for there was a wooden panelling which suggested possibilities.

"Quite clean, Sir."

"No vermin?"

"The officers of the garrison come sometimes."

This took some thinking out. It had an ugly sound, but I gathered that she meant that there could be no question about the cleanliness since these gentlemen were satisfied. So the bargain was struck, and I ordered tea to be ready in an hour, while I went back to the station to fetch up my luggage. A porter brought it up for eightpence (saving fourpence on a cab, my boy!) and so I found myself in the heart of Birchespool with a base of operations secured. I looked out of the little window of my lodgings at the reeking pots and grey sloping roofs, with a spire or two spurting up among them, and I shook my teaspoon defiantly at them. "You've got to conquer me," said I, "or else I'm man enough to conquer you."

Now, you would hardly expect that a fellow would have an adventure on his very first night in a strange town; but I had - a trivial one, it is true, but fairly exciting while it lasted. Certainly it reads more like what might happen to a man in a book, but you may take it from me that it worked out just as I set it down here.

When I had finished my tea, I wrote a few letters - one to Cullingworth, and one to Horton. Then, as it was a lovely evening, I determined to stroll out and see what sort of a place it was upon which Fate had washed me up. "Best begin as you mean to go on," thought I; so I donned my frock-coat, put on my carefully-brushed top-hat, and sallied forth with my very respectable metal-headed walking stick in my hand.

I walked down to the Park, which is the chief centre of the place, and I found that I liked everything I saw of it. It was a lovely evening, and the air was fresh and sweet. I sat down and listened to the band for an hour, watching all the family parties, and feeling particularly lonely. Music nearly always puts me into the minor key; so there came a time when I could stand it no longer, and I set off to find my way back to my lodgings. On the whole, I felt that Birchespool was a place in which a man might very well spend a happy life.

At one end of Cadogan Terrace (where I am lodging) there is a wide open space where several streets meet. In the centre of this stands a large lamp in the middle of a broad stone pedestal, a foot or so high, and ten or twelve across. Well, as I strolled along I saw there was something going on round this lamppost. A crowd of people had gathered, with a swirl in the centre. I was, of course, absolutely determined not to get mixed up in any row; but I could not help pushing my way through the crowd to see what was the matter.

It wasn't a pretty sight. A woman, pinched and bedraggled, with a baby on her arm, was being knocked about by a burly brute of a fellow whom I judged to be her husband from the way in which he cherished her. He was one of those red-faced, dark-eyed men who can look peculiarly malignant when they choose. It was clear that he was half mad with drink, and that she had been trying to lure him away from some den. I was just in time to see him take a flying kick at her, amid cries of "Shame! "from the crowd, and then lurch forward again, with the evident intention of having another, the mob still expostulating vaguely.

If, Bertie, it had been old student days, I should have sailed straight in, as you or any other fellow would have done. My flesh crept with my loathing for the brute. But I had also to think of what I was and where I was, and what I had come there to do. However, there are some things which a man cannot stand, so I took a couple of steps forward, put my hand on the fellow's shoulder, and said in as conciliatory and genial a voice as I could muster: "Come, come, my lad! Pull yourself together."

Instead of "pulling himself together," he very nearly knocked me asunder. I was all abroad for an instant. He had turned on me like a flash, and had struck me on the throat just under the chin, my head being a little back at the moment. It made me swallow once or twice, I can tell you. Sudden as the blow was, I had countered, in the automatic sort of way that a man who knows anything of boxing does. It was only from the elbow, with no body behind it, but it served to stave him off for the moment, while I was making inquiries about my windpipe. Then in he came with a rush; and the crowd swarming round with shrieks of delight, we were pushed, almost locked in each other's arms on to that big pedestal of which I have spoken. "Go it, little 'un!" "Give him beans!" yelled the mob, who had lost all sight of the origin of the fray, and could only see that my opponent was two inches the shorter man. So there, my dear Bertie, was I, within a few hours of my entrance into this town, with my top-hat down to my ears, my highly professional frock-coat, and my kid gloves, fighting some low bruiser on a pedestal in one of the most public places, in the heart of a yelling and hostile mob! I ask you whether that was cruel luck or not?

Cullingworth told me before I started that Birchespool was a lively place. For the next few minutes it struck me as the liveliest I had ever seen. The fellow was a round hand hitter, but so strong that he needed watching. A round blow is, as you know, more dangerous than a straight one if it gets home; for the angle of the jaw, the ear, and the temple, are the three weakest points which you present. However, I took particular care that my man did not get home; but, on the other hand, I fear that I did not do him much harm either. He bored in with his head down; and I, like a fool, broke my knuckles over the top of his impenetrable skull. Of course, theoretically I should either have stepped back and tried an undercut, or else taken him into chancery; but I must confess to feeling flurried and rattled from the blow I had had, as well as from the suddenness of the whole affair. However, I was cooling down, and I daresay should in time have done something rational, when the affray came to a sudden and unexpected end.

This was from the impatience and excitement of the

Sir A. C. Doyle

crowd. The folk behind, wishing to see all that was going on, pushed against those in front, until half-a-dozen of the foremost (with, I think, a woman among them) were flung right up against us. One of these, a rough, sailor-like fellow in a jersey, got wedged between us; and my antagonist, in his blind rage, got one of his swinging blows home upon this new-comer's ear. "What, you - - !" yelled the sailor; and in an instant he had taken over the whole contract, and was at it hammer and tongs with my beauty. I grabbed my stick, which had fallen among the crowd, and backed my way out, rather dishevelled, but very glad to get off so cheaply. From the shouting which I could hear some time after I reached the door of my lodgings, I gathered that a good battle was still raging.

You see, it was the merest piece of luck in the world that my first appearance in Birchespool was not in the dock of the police-court. I should have had no one to answer for me, if I had been arrested, and should have been put quite on a level with my adversary. I daresay you think I made a great fool of myself, but I should like to know how I could have acted otherwise. The only thing that I feel now is my loneliness. What a lucky fellow you are with your wife and child!

After all, I see more and more clearly that both men and women are incomplete, fragmentary, mutilated creatures, as long as they are single. Do what they may to persuade themselves that their state is the happiest, they are still full of vague unrests, of dim, ill-defined dissatisfactions, of a tendency to narrow ways and selfish thoughts. Alone each is a half-made being, with every instinct and feeling yearning for its missing moiety. Together they form a complete and symmetrical whole, the minds of each strongest where that of the other needs reinforcing. I often think that if our souls survive death (and I believe they do, though I base my believe on very different grounds from yours), every male soul will have a female one attached to or combined with it, to round it off and give it symmetry. So thought the old Mormon, you remember, who used it as an argument for his creed. "You cannot take your railway stocks into the next world with you," he said. "But with all our wives and children we should make a good start in the world to come."

I daresay you are smiling at me, as you read this, from the vantage ground of your two years of matrimony. It will be long before I shall be able to put my views into practice.

Well, good-bye, my dear old chap! As I said at the beginning of my letter, the very thought of you is good for me, and never more so than at this moment, when I am alone in a strange city, with very dubious prospects, and an uncertain future. We differ as widely as the poles, you and I, and have done ever since I have known you. You are true to your faith, I to my reason - you to your family belief, I to my own ideas; but our friendship shows that the real essentials of a man, and his affinity for others, depends upon quite other things than views on abstract questions. Anyway, I can say with all my heart that I wish I saw you with that old corncob of yours between your teeth, sitting in that ricketty American-leather armchair, with the villanous lodging-house antimacassar over the back of it. It is good of you to tell me how interested you are in my commonplace adventures; though if I had not KNOWN that you were so, you may be sure that I should never have ventured to inflict any of them upon you. My future is now all involved in obscurity, but it is obvious that the first thing I must do is to find a fitting house, and my second to cajole the landlord into letting me enter into possession of it without any prepayment. To that I will turn myself to-morrow morning, and you shall know the result. Whom should I hear from the other day but Archie McLagan? Of course it was a begging letter. You can judge how far I am in a state to lose money; but in a hot fit I sent him ten shillings, which now, in my cold, I bitterly regret. With every good wish to you and yours, including your town, your State, and your great country, yours as ever.

XI.

1 OAKLEY VILLAS, BIRCHESPOOL,
29th May, 1882.

Birchespool is really a delightful place, dear Bertie; and I ought to know something about it, seeing that I have padded a good hundred miles through its streets during the last seven days. Its mineral springs used to be quite the mode a century or more ago; and it retains many traces of its aristocratic past, carrying it with a certain grace, too, as an emigre countess might wear the faded dress which had once rustled in Versailles. I forget the new roaring suburbs with their out-going manufactures and their incoming wealth, and I live in the queer health-giving old city of the past. The wave of fashion has long passed over it, but a deposit of dreary respectability has been left behind. In the High Street you can see the long iron extinguishers upon the railings where the link-boys used to put out their torches, instead of stamping upon them or slapping them on the pavement, as was the custom in less high-toned quarters. There are the very high curbstones too, so that Lady Teazle or Mrs. Sneerwell could step out of coach or sedan chair without soiling her dainty satin shoes. It brings home to me what an unstable chemical compound man is. Here are the stage accessories as good as ever, while the players have all split up into hydrogen and oxygen and nitrogen and carbon, with traces of iron and silica and phosphorus. A tray full of chemicals and three buckets of water, - there is the raw material of my lady in the sedan chair! It's a curious double picture, if one could but conjure it up. On the one side, the high-born bucks, the mincing ladies, the scheming courtiers, pushing and planning, and striving every one of them to attain his own petty object. Then for a jump of a hundred years. What is this in the corner of the old vault? Margarine and chlesterine, carbonates, sulphates, and ptomaines! We turn from it in loathing, and as we go we carry with us that from which we fly.

But, mind you, Bertie, I have a very high respect for the human body, and I hold that it has been unduly snubbed and maligned by divines and theologians: "our gross frames" and "our miserable mortal clay" are phrases which to my mind partake more of blasphemy than of piety. It is no compliment to the Creator to depreciate His handiwork. Whatever theory or belief we may hold about the soul, there can, I suppose, be no doubt that the body is immortal. Matter may be transformed (in which case it may be re-transformed), but it can never be destroyed. If a comet were to strike this globule of ours, and to knock it into a billion fragments, which were splashed all over the solar system - if its fiery breath were to lick up the earth's surface until it was peeled like an orange, still at the end of a hundred millions of years every tiniest particle of our bodies would exist - in other forms and combinations, it is true, but still those very atoms which now form the forefinger which traces these words. So the child with the same wooden bricks will build a wall, then strew them on the table; then a tower, then strew once more, and so ever with the same bricks.

But then our individuality? I often wonder whether something of that wilt cling to our atoms - whether the dust of Johnnie Munro will ever have something of him about it, and be separable from that of Bertie Swanborough. I think it is possible that we DO impress ourselves upon the units of our own structure. There are facts which tend to show that every tiny organic cell of which a man is composed, contains in its microcosm a complete miniature of the individual of which it forms a part. The ovum itself from which we are all produced is, as you know, too small to be transfixed upon the point of a fine needle; and yet within that narrow globe lies the potentiality, not only for reproducing the features of two individuals, but even their smallest tricks of habit and of thought. Well, if a single cell contains so much, perhaps a single molecule and atom has more than we think.

Have you ever had any personal experience of dermoid cysts? We had one in Cullingworth's practice just before his illness, and we were both much excited about it. They seem to me to be one of those wee little chinks through which one may see deep into Nature's workings. In this case the fellow, who was a clerk in the post office, came to us with a swelling over his eyebrow. We opened it under the impression that it was an abscess, and found inside some hair and a rudimentary jaw with teeth in it. You know that such cases are common enough in surgery, and that no pathological museum is without an example.

But what are we to understand by it? So startling a phenomenon must have a deep meaning. That can only be, I think, that EVERY cell in the body has the power latent in it by which it may reproduce the whole individual - and that occasionally under some special circumstances - some obscure nervous or vascular excitement - one of these microscopic units of structure actually does make a clumsy attempt in that direction.

But, my goodness, where have I got to? All this comes from the Birchespool lamp-posts and curb-stones. And I sat down to write such a practical letter too! However, I give you leave to be as dogmatic and didactic as you like in return. Cullingworth says my head is like a bursting capsule, with all the seeds getting loose. Poor seed, too, I fear, but some of it may lodge somewhere - or not, as Fate pleases.

I wrote to you last on the night that I reached here. Next morning I set to work upon my task. You would be surprised (at least I was) to see how practical and methodical I can be. First of all I walked down to the post-office and I bought a large shilling map of the town. Then back I came and pinned this out upon the lodging-house table. This done, I set to work to study it, and to arrange a series of walks by which I should pass through every street of the place. You have no idea what that means until you try to do it. I used to have breakfast, get out about ten, walk till one, have a cheap luncheon (I can do well on three-pence), walk till four, get back and note results. On my map I put a cross for every empty house and a circle for every doctor. So at the end of that time I had a complete chart of the whole place, and could see at a glance where there was a possible opening, and what opposition there was at each point.

In the meantime I had enlisted a most unexpected ally. On the second evening a card was solemnly brought up by the landlady's daughter from the lodger who occupied the room below. On it was inscribed "Captain Whitehall"; and then underneath, in brackets, "Armed Transport." On the back of the card was written, "Captain Whitehall (Armed Transport) presents his compliments to Dr. Munro, and would be glad of his company to supper at 8.30." To this I answered, "Dr. Munro presents his compliments to Captain Whitehall (Armed Transport), and will be most happy to accept his kind invitation." What "Armed Transport" might mean I had not an idea, but I thought it well to include it, as he seemed so particular about it himself.

On descending I found a curious-looking figure in a gray dressing-gown with a purple cord. He was an elderly man - his hair not quite white yet, but well past mouse colour. His beard and moustache, however, were of a yellowish brown, and his face all puckered and shot with wrinkles, spare and yet puffy, with hanging bags under his singular light blue eyes.

"By God, Dr. Munro, sir," said he, as he shook my hand. "I take it as very kind of you that you should accept an informal invitation. I do, sir, by God!"

This sentence was, as it proved, a very typical one, for he nearly always began and ended each with an oath, while the centre was, as a rule, remarkable for a certain suave courtesy. So regular was his formula that I may omit it and you suppose it, every time that he opened his mouth. A dash here and there will remind you.

It's been my practice, Dr. Munro, sir, to make friends with my neighbours through life; and some strange neighbours I have had. By -- , sir, humble as you see me, I have sat with a general on my right, and an admiral on my left, and my toes up against a British ambassador.

That was when I commanded the armed transport Hegira in the Black Sea in '55. Burst up in the great gale in Balaclava Bay, sir, and not as much left as you could pick your teeth with."

There was a strong smell of whisky in the room, and an uncorked bottle upon the mantelpiece. The captain himself spoke with a curious stutter, which I put down at first to a natural defect; but his lurch as he, turned back to his armchair showed me that he had had as much as he could carry.

"Not much to offer you, Dr. Munro, sir. The hind leg of a -- duck, and a sailor's welcome. Not Royal Navy, sir, though I have a -- sight better manners than many that are. No, sir, I fly no false colours, and put no R. N. after my name; but I'm the Queen's servant, by --! No mercantile marine about me! Have a wet, sir! It's the right stuff, and I have drunk enough to know the difference."

Well, as the supper progressed I warmed with the liquor and the food, and I told my new acquaintance all about my plans and intentions. I didn't realise how lonely I had been until I found the pleasure of talking. He listened to it all with much sympathy, and to my horror tossed off a whole tumbler-full of neat whisky to my success. So enthusiastic was he that it was all I could do to prevent him from draining a second one.

"You'll do it, Dr. Munro, sir!" he cried. "I know a man when I see one, and you'll do it. There's my hand, sir! I'm with you! You needn't be ashamed to grasp it, for by --, though I say it myself, it's been open to the poor and shut to a bully ever since I could suck milk. Yes, sir, you'll make a good ship-mate, and I'm -- glad to have you on my poop.

For the remainder of the evening his fixed delusion was that I had come to serve under him; and he read me long rambling lectures about ship's discipline, still always addressing me as "Dr. Munro. sir." At last, however, his conversation became unbearable - a foul young man is odious, but a foul old one is surely the most sickening thing on earth. One feels that the white upon the hair, like that upon the mountain, should signify a height attained. I rose and bade him good-night, with a last impression of him leaning back in his dressing-gown, a sodden cigar-end in the corner of his mouth, his beard all slopped with whisky, and his half-glazed eyes looking sideways after me with the leer of a satyr. I had to go into the street and walk up and down for half-an-hour before I felt clean enough to go to bed.

Well, I wanted to see no more of my neighbour, but in he came as I was sitting at breakfast, smelling like a bar-parlour, with stale whisky oozing at every pore.

"Good morning, Dr. Munro, sir," said he, holding out a twitching hand. "I compliment you, sir! You look fresh, -- fresh, and me with a head like a toy-shop. We had a pleasant, quiet evening, and I took nothing to hurt, but it is the -- relaxing air of this place that settles me. I can't bear up against it. Last year it gave me the horrors, and I expect it will again. You're off house-hunting, I suppose?"

"I start immediately after breakfast."

"I take a cursed interest in the whole thing. You may think it a -- impertinence, but that's the way I'm made. As long as I can steam I'll throw a rope to whoever wants a tow. I'll tell you what I'll do, Dr. Munro, sir. I'll stand on one tack if you'll stand on the other, and I'll let you know if I come across anything that will do."

There seemed to be no alternative between taking him with me, or letting him go alone; so I could only thank him and let him have carte blanche. Every night he would turn up, half-drunk as a rule, having, I believe, walked his ten or fifteen miles as conscientiously as I had done. He came with the most grotesque suggestions.

Once he had actually entered into negotiations with the owner of a huge shop, a place that had been a raper's, with a counter about sixty feet long. His reason was that he knew an innkeeper who had done very well a little further down on the other side. Poor old "armed transport" worked so hard that I could not help being touched and grateful; yet I longed from my heart that he would stop for he was a most unsavoury agent, and I never knew what extraordinary step he might take in my name. He introduced me to two other men, one of them a singular-looking creature named Turpey, who was struggling along upon a wound-pension, having, when only a senior midshipman, lost the sight of one eye and the use of one arm through the injuries he received at some unpronounceable Pah in the Maori war. The other was a sad-faced poetical-looking man, of good birth as I understood, who had been disowned by his family on the occasion of his eloping with the cook. His name was Carr, and his chief peculiarity, that he was so regular in his irregularities that he could always tell the time of day by the state of befuddlement that he was in. He would cock his head, think over his own symptoms, and then give you the hour fairly correctly. An unusual drink would disarrange him, however; and if you forced the pace in the morning, he would undress and go to bed about tea-time, with a full conviction that all the clocks had gone mad. These two strange waifs were among the craft to whom old Whitehall had in his own words, "thrown a rope"; and long after I had gone to bed I could hear the clink of their glasses, and the tapping of their pipes against the fender in the room below.

Well, when I had finished my empty-house-and-doctor chart, I found that there was one villa to let, which undoubtedly was far the most suitable for my purpose. In the first place it was fairly cheap-forty pounds, or fifty with taxes. The front looked well. It had no garden. It stood with the well-to-do quarter upon the one side, and the poorer upon the other. Finally, it was almost at the intersection of four roads, one of which was a main artery of the town. Altogether, if I had ordered a house for my purpose I could hardly have got anything better, and I was thrilled with apprehension lest some one should get before me to the agent. I hurried round and burst into the office with a precipitancy which rather startled the demure clerk inside.

His replies, however, were reassuring. The house was still to let. It was not quite the quarter yet, but I could enter into possession. I must sign an agreement to take it for one year, and it was usual to pay a quarter's rent in advance.

I don't know whether I turned colour a little.

"In advance!" I said, as carelessly as I could.

"It is usual."

"Or references?"

"Well, that depends, of couse{sic}, upon the references."

"Not that it matters much," said I. (Heaven forgive me!) "Still, if it is the same to the firm, I may as well pay by the quarter, as I shall do afterwards."

"What names did you propose to give?" he asked.

My heart gave a bound, for I knew that all was right. My uncle, as you know, won his knighthood in the Artillery, and though I have seen nothing of him, I knew that he was the man to pull me out of this tight corner.

"There's my uncle, Sir Alexander Munro, Lismore House, Dublin," said I. "He would be happy to answer any inquiry, and so would my friend Dr. Cullingworth of Bradfield."

I brought him down with both barrels. I could see it by his eyes and the curve of his back.

"I have no doubt that that will be quite satisfactory," said he. "Perhaps you would kindly sign the agreement."

I did so, and drew my hind foot across the Rubicon. The die was cast. Come what might, 1 Oakley Villas was on my hand for a twelve-month.

"Would you like the key now?"

I nearly snatched it out of his hands. Then away I ran to take possession of my property. Never shall I forget my feelings, my dear Bertie, when the key clicked in the lock, and the door flew open. It was my own house - all my very own! I shut the door again, the noise of the street died down, and I had, in that empty, dust-strewn hall, such a sense of soothing privacy as had never come to me before. In all my life it was the first time that I had ever stood upon boards which were not paid for by another.

Then I proceeded to go from room to room with a delicious sense of exploration. There were two upon the ground floor, sixteen feet square each, and I saw with satisfaction that the wall papers were in fair condition. The front one would make a consulting room, the other a waiting room, though I did not care to reflect who was most likely to do the waiting. I was in the highest spirits, and did a step dance in each room as an official inauguration.

Then down a winding wooden stair to the basement, where were kitchen and scullery, dimly lit, and asphalt-floored. As I entered the latter I stood staring. In every corner piles of human jaws were grinning at me. The place was a Golgotha! In that half light the effect was sepulchral. But as I approached and picked up one of them the mystery vanished. They were of plaster-of-Paris, and were the leavings evidently of the dentist, who had been the last tenant. A more welcome sight was a huge wooden dresser with drawers and a fine cupboard in the corner. It only wanted a table and a chair to be a furnished room.

Sir A. C. Doyle

Then I ascended again and went up the first flight of stairs. There were two other good sized apartments there. One should be my bedroom, and the other a spare room. And then another flight with two more. One for the servant, when I had one, and the other for a guest.

From the windows I had a view of the undulating gray back of the city, with the bustle of green tree tops. It was a windy day, and the clouds were drifting swiftly across the heavens, with glimpses of blue between. I don't know how it was, but as I stood looking through the grimy panes in the empty rooms a sudden sense of my own individuality and of my responsibility to some higher power came upon me, with a vividness which was overpowering. Here was a new chapter of my life about to be opened. What was to be the end of it? I had strength, I had gifts. What was I going to do with them? All the world, the street, the cabs, the houses, seemed to fall away, and the mite of a figure and the unspeakable Guide of the Universe were for an instant face to face. I was on my knees - hurled down all against my own will, as it were. And even then I could find no words to say. Only vague yearnings and emotions and a heartfelt wish to put my shoulder to the great wheel of good. What could I say? Every prayer seemed based on the idea that God was a magnified man - that He needed asking and praising and thanking. Should the cog of the wheel creak praise to the Engineer? Let it rather cog harder, and creak less. Yet I did, I confess, try to put the agitation of my soul into words. I meant it for a prayer; but when I considered afterwards the "supposing thats" and "in case ofs" with which it was sprinkled, it must have been more like a legal document. And yet I felt soothed and happier as I went downstairs again.

I tell you this, Bertie, because if I put reason above emotion I would not have you think that I am not open to attacks of the latter also. I feel that what I say about religion is too cold and academic. I feel that there should be something warmer and sweeter and more comforting. But if you ask me to buy this at the price of making myself believe a thing to be true, which all that is nearest the divine in me cries out against, then you are selling your opiates too high. I'm a volunteer for "God's own forlorn hope," and I'll clamber up the breech as long as I think I can see the flag of truth waving in front of me.

Well, my next two cares were to get drugs and furniture. The former I was sure that I could obtain on long credit; while the latter I was absolutely determined not to get into debt over. I wrote to the Apothecaries' Company, giving the names of Cullingworth and of my father, and ordering twelve pounds' worth of tinctures, infusions, pills, powders, ointments, and bottles. Cullingworth must, I should think, have been one of their very largest customers, so I knew very well that my order would meet with prompt attention.

There remained the more serious matter of the furniture. I calculated that when my lodgings were paid for I might, without quite emptying my purse, expend four pounds upon furniture - not a large allowance for a good sized villa. That would leave me a few shillings to go on with, and before they were exhausted Cullingworth's pound would come in. Those pounds, however, would be needed for the rent, so I could hardly reckon upon them at all, as far as my immediate wants went. I found in the columns of the Birchespool Post that there was to be a sale of furniture that evening, and I went down to the auctioneer's rooms, accompanied, much against my will, by Captain Whitehall, who was very drunk and affectionate.

"By God, Dr. Munro, sir, I'm the man that's going to stick to you. I'm only an old sailor-man, sir, with perhaps more liquor than sense; but I'm the Queen's servant, and touch my pension every quarter day. I don't claim to be R. N., but I'm not merchant service either. Here I am, rotting in lodgings, but by --, Dr. Munro, sir, I carried seven thousand stinking Turks from Varna to Balaclava Bay. I'm with you, Dr. Munro, and we put this thing through together."

We came to the auction rooms and we stood on the fringe of the crowd waiting for our chance. Presently up went a very neat little table. I gave a nod and got it for nine shillings. Then three rather striking looking chairs, black wood and cane bottoms. Four shillings each I gave for those. Then a metal umbrella-stand, four and sixpence. That was a mere luxury, but I was warming to the work. A job lot of curtains all tied together in a bundle went up. Somebody bid five shillings. The auctioneer's eye came round to me, and I nodded. Mine again for five and sixpence. Then I bought a square of red drugget for half-a-crown, a small iron bed for nine shillings, three watercolour paintings, "Spring," "The Banjo Player," and "Windsor Castle," for five shillings; a tiny fender, half-a-crown; a toilet set, five shillings; another very small square-topped table, three and sixpence. Whenever I bid for anything, Whitehall thrust his black-thorn up into the air, and presently I found him doing so on my behalf when I had no intention of buying. I narrowly escaped having to give fourteen and sixpence for a stuffed macaw in a glass case.

"It would do to hang in your hall, Dr. Munro, sir," said he when I remonstrated with him.

"I should have to hang myself in my hall soon if I spent my money like that," said I. "I've got as much as I can afford now, and I must stop."

When the auction was over, I paid my bill and had my goods hoisted on to a trolly, the porter undertaking to deliver them for two shillings. I found that I had over-estimated the cost of furnishing, for the total expense was little more than three pounds. We walked round to Oakley Villa, and I proudly deposited all my goods in the hall. And here came another extraordinary example of the kindness of the poorer classes. The porter when I had paid him went out to his trolly and returned with a huge mat of oakum, as ugly a thing as I have ever set eyes upon. This he laid down inside my door, and then without a word, brushing aside every remonstrance or attempt at thanks, he vanished away with his trolly into the night.

Next morning I came round to my house - MY house, my boy! - for good and all, after paying off my landlady. Her bill came to more than I expected, for I only had breakfast and tea, always "dining out" as I majestically expressed it. However, it was a relief to me to get it settled, and to go round with my box to Oakley Villas. An ironmonger had fixed my plate on to the railings for half-a-crown the evening before, and there it was, glittering in the sun, when I came round. It made me quite shy to look at it, and I slunk into the house with a feeling that every window in the street had a facein it.

But once inside, there was so much to be done that I

Sir A. C. Doyle

did not know what I should turn to first. I bought a one-and-ninepenny broom and set to work. You notice that I am precise about small sums, because just there lies the whole key of the situation. In the yard I found a zinc pail with a hole in it, which was most useful, for by its aid I managed to carry up all the jaws with which my kitchen was heaped. Then with my new broom, my coat hung on a gas-bracket and my shirt sleeves turned to the elbow, I cleaned out the lower rooms and the hall, brushing the refuse into the yard. After that I did as much for the upper floor, with the result that I brought several square yards of dust down into the hall again, and undid my previous cleaning. This was disheartening, but at least it taught me to begin at the furthest point in future. When I had finished, I was as hot and dirty as if it were half-time at a football match. I thought of our tidy charwoman at home, and realised what splendid training she must be in.

Then came the arranging of the furniture. The hall was easily managed, for the planks were of a dark colour, which looked well of themselves. My oakum mat and my umbrella stand were the only things in it; but I bought three pegs for sixpence, and fastened them up at the side, completing the effect by hanging my two hats up on them. Finally, as the expanse of bare floor was depressing, I fixed one of my curtains about halfway down it, draping it back, so that it had a kind of oriental look, and excited a vague idea of suites of apartments beyond. It was a fine effect, and I was exceedingly proud of it.

From that I turned to the most important point of all - the arrangement of my consulting room. My experience with Cullingworth had taught me one thing at least, - that patients care nothing about your house if they only think that you can cure them. Once get that idea into their heads, and you may live in a vacant stall in a stable and write your prescriptions on the manger. Still, as this was, for many a day to come, to be the only furnished room in my house, it was worth a little planning to get it set out to the best advantage.

My red drugget I laid out in the centre, and fastened it down with brass-headed nails. It looked much smaller than I had hoped, - a little red island on an ocean of deal board, or a postage stamp in the middle of an envelope. In the centre of it I placed my table, with three medical works on one side of it, and my stethoscope and dresser's case upon the other. One chair went with the table, of course; and then I spent the next ten minutes in trying to determine whether the other two looked better together - a dense block of chairs, as it were - or scattered so that the casual glance would get the idea of numerous chairs. I placed them finally one on the right, and one in front of the table. Then I put down my fender, and nailed "Spring," "The Banjo Players," and "Windsor Castle" on to three of the walls, with the mental promise that my first spare half-crown should buy a picture for the fourth. In the window I placed my little square table, and balanced upon it a photograph with an ivory mounting and a nice plush frame which I had brought in my trunk. Finally, I found a pair of dark brown curtains among the job lot which I had bought at the sale, and these I put up and drew pretty close together, so that a subdued light came into the room, which toned everything down, and made the dark corners look furnished. When I had finished I really do not believe that any one could have guessed that the total contents of that room came to about thirty shillings.

Sir A. C. Doyle

Then I pulled my iron bed upstairs and fixed it in the room which I had from the first determined upon as my bedchamber. I found an old packing case in the yard - a relic of my predecessor's removal - and this made a very good wash-hand stand for my basin and jug. When it was all fixed up I walked, swelling with pride, through my own chambers, giving a touch here and a touch there until I had it perfect. I wish my mother could see it - or, on second thoughts, I don't; for I know that her first act would be to prepare gallons of hot water, and to holystone the whole place down, from garret to cellar - and I know by my own small experience what that means.

Well, that's as far as I've got as yet. What trivial, trivial stuff, interesting to hardly a soul under heaven, save only about three! Yet it pleases me to write as long as I have your assurance that it pleases you to read. Pray, give my kindest remembrances to your wife, and to Camelford also, if he should happen to come your way. He was on the Mississippi when last I heard.

XII.

1 OAKLEY VILLAS, BIRCHESPOOL,
5th June, 1882.

When I had made all those dispositions which I described with such painful prolixity in my last letter, my dear Bertie, I sat down on my study chair, and I laid out the whole of my worldly wealth upon the table in front of me. I was startled when I looked at it, - three half-crowns, a florin, and four sixpences, or eleven and sixpence in all. I had expected to hear from Cullingworth before this; but at least he was always there, a trusty friend, at my back. Immediately upon engaging the house I had written him a very full letter, telling him that I had committed myself to keeping it for one year, but assuring him that I was quite convinced that with the help which he had promised me I should be able to hold my own easily. I described the favourable position of the house, and gave him every detail of the rent and neighbourhood. That letter would, I was sure, bring a reply from him which would contain my weekly remittance. One thing I had, above all, determined upon. That was that, whatever hard- ships might lie before me, I would fight through them without help from home. I knew, of course, that my mother would have sold everything down to her gold eye-glasses to help me, and that no thought of our recent disagreement would have weighed with her for an instant; but still a man has his feelings, you know,

Sir A. C. Doyle

and I did not propose to act against her judgment and then run howling for help.

I sat in my house all day, with that ever-present sense of privacy and novelty which had thrilled me when I first shut the street door behind me. At evening I sallied out and bought a loaf of bread, half a pound of tea ("sweepings," they call it, and it cost eightpence), a tin kettle (fivepence), a pound of sugar, a tin of Swiss milk, and a tin of American potted meat. I had often heard my mother groan over the expenses of housekeeping, and now I began to understand what she meant. Two and ninepence went like a flash, but at least I had enough to keep myself going for some days.

There was a convenient gas bracket in the back room. I hammered a splinter of wood into the wall above it, and so made an arm upon which I could hang my little kettle and boil it over the flame. The attraction of the idea was that there was no immediate expense, and many things would have happened before I was called upon to pay the gas bill. The back room was converted then into both kitchen and dining room. The sole furniture consisted of my box, which served both as cupboard, as table, and as chair. My eatables were all kept inside, and when I wished for a meal I had only to pick them out and lay them on the lid, leaving room for myself to sit beside them.

It was only when I went to my bedroom that I realised the oversights which I had made in my furnishing. There was no mattress and no pillow or bed-clothes. My mind had been so centred upon the essentials for the practice, that I had never given a thought to my own private wants. I slept that night upon the irons of my bed, and rose up like St. Lawrence from the gridiron. My second suit of clothes with Bristowe's "Principles of Medicine" made an excellent pillow, while on a warm June night a man can do well wrapped in his overcoat. I had no fancy for second-hand bed-clothes, and determined until I could buy some new ones, to make myself a straw pillow, and to put on both my suits of clothes on the colder nights. Two days later, however, the problem was solved in more luxurious style by the arrival of a big brown tin box from my mother, which was as welcome to me, and as much of a windfall, as the Spanish wreck to Robinson Crusoe. There were too pairs of thick blankets, two sheets, a counterpane, a pillow, a camp-stool, two stuffed bears' paws (of all things in this world!), two terra-cotta vases, a tea-cosy, two pictures in frames, several books, an ornamental ink-pot, and a number of antimacassars and coloured tablecloths. It is not until you own a table with a deal top and mahogany legs, that you understand what the true inner meaning of an ornamental cloth is. Right on the top of this treasure came a huge hamper from the Apothecaries' Society with the drugs which I had ordered. When they were laid out in line, the bottles extended right down one side of the dining-room and half down the other. As I walked through my house and viewed my varied possessions, I felt less radical in my views, and begun to think that there might be something in the rights of property after all.

And I added to my effects in a marvellous way. I made myself an excellent mattress out of some sacking and the straw in which the medicine bottles had been packed.

Again, out of three shutters which belonged to the room, I rigged up a very effective side-table for my own den, which when covered with a red cloth, and ornamented with the bears' paws, might have cost twenty guineas for all that the patient could say to the contrary. I had done all this with a light heart and a good spirit before the paralysing blow which I shall have to tell you about, came upon me.

Of course it was obvious from the first that a servant was out of the question. I could not feed one, far less pay one, and I had no kitchen furniture. I must open my door to my own patients - let them think what they would of it. I must clean my own plate and brush down my own front; and these duties must be thoroughly done, come what might, for I must show a presentable outside to the public. Well, there was no great hardship in that, for I could do it under the cover of night. But I had had a suggestion from my mother which simplified matters immensely. She had written to say that if I wished she would send my little brother Paul to keep me company. I wrote back eagerly to agree. He was a hardy cheery little fellow of nine, who would, I knew, gladly share hard times with me; while, if they became unduly so, I could always have him taken home again. Some weeks must pass before he could come, but it cheered me to think of him. Apart from his company, there were a thousand ways in which he might be useful.

Who should come in on the second day but old Captain Whitehall? I was in the back room, trying how many slices I could make out of a pound of potted beef, when he rang my bell, and I only just shut my mouth in time to prevent my heart jumping out.

How that bell clanged through the empty house! I saw who it was, however, when I went into the hall; for the middle panels of my door are of glazed glass, so that I can always study a silhouette of my visitors before coming to closer quarters.

I was not quite sure yet whether I loathed the man or liked him. He was the most extraordinary mixture of charity and drunkenness, lechery and self-sacrifice that I had ever come across. But he brought into the house with him a whiff of cheeriness and hope for which I could not but be grateful. He had a large brown paper parcel under his arm, which he unwrapped upon my table, displaying a great brown jar. This he carried over and deposited on the centre of my mantel-piece.

"You will permit me, Dr. Munro, sir, to place this trifle in your room. It's lava, sir; lava from Vesuvius, and made in Naples. By -- , you may think its empty, Dr. Munro, sir, but it is full of my best wishes; and when you've got the best practice in this town you may point to that vase and tell how it came from a skipper of an armed transport, who backed you from the start."

I tell you, Bertie, the tears started to my eyes, and I could hardly gulp out a word or two of thanks. What a crisscross of qualities in one human soul! It was not the deed or the words; but it was the almost womanly look in the eyes of this broken, drink-sodden old Bohemian - the sympathy and the craving for sympathy which I read there. Only for an instant though, for he hardened again into his usual reckless and half defiant manner.

"There's another thing, sir. I've been thinking for some time back of having a medical opinion on myself. I'd be glad to put myself under your hands, if you would take a survey of me."

"What's the matter?" I asked.

"Dr. Munro, sir," said he, "I am a walking museum. You could fit what ISN'T the matter with me on to the back of a -- visiting card. If there's any complaint you want to make a special study of, just you come to me, sir, and see what I can do for you. It's not every one that can say that he has had cholera three times, and cured himself by living on red pepper and brandy. If you can only set the -- little germs sneezing they'll soon leave you alone. That's my theory about cholera, and you should make a note of it, Dr. Munro, sir, for I was shipmates with fifty dead men when I was commanding the armed transport Hegira in the Black Sea, and I know -- well what I am talking about."

I fill in Whitehall's oaths with blanks because I feel how hopeless it is to reproduce their energy and variety. I was amazed when he stripped, for his whole body was covered with a perfect panorama of tattooings, with a big blue Venus right over his heart.

"You may knock," said he, when I began to percuss his chest, "but I am -- sure there's no one at home. They've all gone visiting one another. Sir John Hutton had a try some years ago. `Why, dammy, man, where's your liver?' said he. `Seems to me that some one has stirred you up with a porridge stick,' said he. `Nothing is in its right place.' `Except my heart, Sir John,' said I. `Aye, by --, that will never lose its moorings while it has a flap left.'"

Well, I examined him, and I found his own account not very far from the truth. I went over him carefully from head to foot, and there was not much left as Nature made it. He had mitral regurgitation, cirrhosis of the liver, Bright's disease, an enlarged spleen, and incipient dropsy. I gave him a lecture about the necessity of temperance, if not of total abstinence; but I fear that my words made no impression. He chuckled, and made a kind of clucking noise in his throat all the time that I was speaking, but whether in assent or remonstrance I cannot say.

He pulled out his purse when I had finished, but I begged him to look on my small service as a mere little act of friendship. This would not do at all, however, and he seemed so determined about it that I was forced to give way.

"My fee is five shillings, then, since you insist upon making it a business matter."

"Dr. Munro, sir," he broke out, "I have been examined by men whom I wouldn't throw a bucket of water over if they were burning, and I never paid them less than a guinea. Now that I have come to a gentleman and a friend, stiffen me purple if I pay one farthing less."

So, after much argument, it ended in the kind fellow going off and leaving a sovereign and a shilling on the edge of my table. The money burned my fingers, for I knew that his pension was not a very large one; and yet, since I could not avoid taking it, there was no denying that it was exceedingly useful. Out I sallied and spent sixteen shillings of it upon a new palliasse which should go under the straw mattress upon my bed. Already, you see, I was getting to a state of enervating luxury in my household arrangements, and I could only lull my conscience by reminding myself that little Paul would have to sleep with me when he came.

However, I had not quite got to the end of Whitehall's visit yet. When I went back I took down the beautiful lava jug, and inside I found his card. On the back was written, "You have gone into action, sir. It may be your fate to sink or to swim, but it can never be your degradation to strike. Die on the last plank and be damned to you, or come into port with your ensign flying mast-high."

Was it not fine? It stirred my blood, and the words rang like a bugle call in my head. It braced me, and the time was coming when all the bracing I could get would not be too much. I copied it out, and pinned it on one side of my mantel-piece. On the other I stuck up a chip from Carlyle, which I daresay is as familiar to you as to me. "One way or another all the light, energy, and available virtue which we have does come out of us, and goes very infallibly into God's treasury, living and working through eternities there. We are not lost - not a single atom of us - of one of us." Now, there is a religious sentence which is intellectually satisfying, and therefore morally sound.

This last quotation leads to my second visitor. Such a row we had! I make a mistake in telling you about it, for I know your sympathies will be against me; but at least it will have the good effect of making you boil over into a letter of remonstrance and argument than which nothing could please me better.

Well, the second person whom I admitted through my door was the High Church curate of the parish - at least, I deduced High Church from his collar and the cross which dangled from his watch chain. He seemed to be a fine upstanding manly fellow - in fact, I am bound in honesty to admit that I have never met the washy tea-party curate outside the pages of Punch. As a body, I think they would compare very well in manliness (I do not say in brains) with as many young lawyers or doctors. Still, I have no love for the cloth. Just as cotton, which is in itself the most harmless substance in the world, becomes dangerous on being dipped into nitric acid, so the mildest of mortals is to be feared if he is once soaked in sectarian religion. If he has any rancour or hardness in him it will bring it out. I was therefore by no means overjoyed to see my visitor, though I trust that I received him with fitting courtesy. The quick little glance of surprise which he shot round him as he entered my consulting-room, told me that it was not quite what he had expected.

"You see, the Vicar has been away for two years," he explained, "and we have to look after things in his absence. His chest is weak, and he can't stand Birches-pool. I live just opposite, and, seeing your plate go up, I thought I would call and welcome you into our parish."

I told him that I was very much obliged for the attention. If he had stopped there all would have been well, and we should have had a pleasant little chat. But I suppose it was his sense of duty which would not permit it.

"I trust," said he, "that we shall see you at St. Joseph's."

I was compelled to explain that it was not probable.

"A Roman Catholic?" he asked, in a not unfriendly voice.

I shook my head, but nothing would discourage him.

"Not a dissenter!" he exclaimed, with a sudden hardening of his genial face.

I shook my head again.

"Ah, a little lax - a little remiss!" he said playfully, and with an expression of relief. "Professional men get into these ways. They have much to distract them. At least, you cling fast, no doubt, to the fundamental truths of Christianity?"

"I believe from the bottom of my heart," said I, "that the Founder of it was the best and sweetest character of whom we have any record in the history of this planet."

But instead of soothing him, my conciliatory answer seemed to be taken as a challenge. "I trust," said he severely, "that your belief goes further than that. You, are surely prepared to admit that He was an incarnation of the God-head."

I began to feel like the old badger in his hole who longs to have a scratch at the black muzzle which is so eager to draw him.

"Does it not strike you," I said, "that if He were but a frail mortal like ourselves, His life assumes a much deeper significance? It then becomes a standard towards which we might work. If, on the other hand, He was intrinsically of a different nature to ourselves, then His existence loses its point, since we and He start upon a different basis. To my mind it is obvious that such a supposition takes away the beauty and the moral of His life. If He was divine then He COULD not sin, and there was an end of the matter. We who are not divine and can sin, have little to learn from a life like that."

"He triumphed over sin," said my visitor, as if a text or a phrase were an argument.

"A cheap triumph!" I said. "You remember that Roman emperor who used to descend into the arena fully armed, and pit himself against some poor wretch who had only a leaden foil which would double up at a thrust. According to your theory of your Master's life, you would have it that He faced the temptations of this world at such an advantage that they were only harmless leaden things, and not the sharp assailants which we find them. I confess, in my own case, that my sympathy is as strong when I think of His weaknesses as of His wisdom and His virtue. They come more home to me, I suppose, since I am weak myself."

"Perhaps you would be good enough to tell me what has impressed you as weak in His conduct?" asked my visitor stiffly.

"Well, the more human traits - `weak' is hardly the word I should have used. His rebuke of the Sabbatarians, His personal violence to the hucksters, His outbursts against the Pharisees, His rather unreasoning petulance against the fig-tree because it bore no fruit at the wrong season of the year, His very human feeling towards the housewife who bustled about when He was talking, his gratification that the ointment should have been used for Him instead of being devoted to the poor, His self-distrust before the crisis - these make me

Sir A. C. Doyle

realize and love the man."

"You are a Unitarian, then, or rather, perhaps, a mere Deist?" said the curate, with a combative flush.

"You may label me as you like," I answered (and by this time I fear that I had got my preaching stop fairly out); "I don't pretend to know what truth is, for it is infinite, and I finite; but I know particularly well what it is NOT. It is not true that religion reached its acme nineteen hundred years ago, and that we are for ever to refer back to what was written and said in those days. No, sir; religion is a vital living thing, still growing and working, capable of endless extension and development, like all other fields of thought. There were many eternal truths spoken of old and handed down to us in a book, some parts of which may indeed be called holy. But there are others yet to be revealed; and if we are to reject them because they are not in those pages, we should act as wisely as the scientist who would take no notice of Kirschoff's spectral analysis because there is no mention of it in Albertus Magnus. A modern prophet may wear a broadcloth coat and write to the magazines; but none the less he may be the little pipe which conveys a tiny squirt from the reservoirs of truth. Look at this!" I cried, rising and reading my Carlyle text. "That comes from no Hebrew prophet, but from a ratepayer in Chelsea. He and Emerson are also among the prophets. The Almighty has not said His last say to the human race, and He can speak through a Scotchman or a New Englander as easily as through a Jew. The Bible, sir, is a book which comes out in instalments, and `To be continued,' not `Finis,' is written at the end of it."

My visitor had been showing every sign of acute

uneasiness during this long speech of mine. Finally, he sprang to his feet, and took his hat from the table.

"Your opinions are highly dangerous, sir," said he. "It is my duty to tell you so. You believe in nothing."

"Nothing which limits the power or the goodness of the Almighty," I answered.

"You have evolved all this from your own spiritual pride and self-sufficiency," said he, hotly. "Why do you not turn to that Deity whose name you use. Why do you not humble yourself before Him?"

"How do you know I don't?"

"You said yourself that you never went to church."

"I carry my own church about under my own hat," said I. "Bricks and mortar won't make a staircase to heaven. I believe with your Master that the human heart is the best temple. I am sorry to see that you differ from Him upon the point."

Perhaps it was too bad of me to say that. I might have guarded without countering. Anyhow; it had the effect of ending an interview which was becoming oppressive. My visitor was too indignant to answer, and swept out of the room without a word. From my window I could see him hurry down the street, a little black angry thing, very hot and troubled because he cannot measure the whole universe with his pocket square and compasses.

Think of it, and think of what he is, an atom among atoms, standing at the meeting point of two eternities!

But what am I, a brother atom, that I should judge him?

After all, I own to you, that it might have been better had I listened to what he had to say, and refused to give my own views. On the other hand, truth MUST be as broad as the universe which it is to explain, and therefore far broader than anything which the mind of man can conceive. A protest against sectarian thought must always be an aspiration towards truth. Who shall dare to claim a monopoly of the Almighty? It would be an insolence on the part of a solar system, and yet it is done every day by a hundred little cliques of mystery mongers. There lies the real impiety.

Well, the upshot of it all is, my dear Bertie, that I have begun my practice by making an enemy of the man who, of the whole parish, has the most power to injure me. I know what my father would think about it, if he knew.

And now I come to the great event of this morning, from which I am still gasping. That villain Cullingworth has cut the painter, and left me to drift as best I may.

My post comes at eight o'clock in the morning, and I usually get my letters and take them into bed to read them. There was only one this morning, addressed in his strange, unmistakable hand. I made sure, of course, that it was my promised remittance, and I opened it with a pleasurable feeling of expectation. This is a copy of what I read: -

"When the maid was arranging your room after your departure, she cleared some pieces of torn paper from under the grate. Seeing my name upon them, she brought them, as in duty bound, to her mistress, who pasted them together and found that they formed a letter from your mother to you, in which I am referred to in the vilest terms, such as `a bankrupt swindler' and `the unscrupulous Cullingworth.' I can only say that we are astonished that you could have been a party to such a correspondence while you were a guest under our roof, and we refuse to have anything more to do with you in any shape or form."

That was a nice little morning greeting was it not, after I had, on the strength of his promise, started in practice, and engaged a house for a year with a few shillings in my pocket? I have given up smoking for reasons of economy; but I felt that the situation was worthy of a pipe, so I climbed out of bed, gathered a little heap of tobacco-dust from the linings of my pocket, and smoked the whole thing over. That life-belt of which I had spoken so confidingly had burst, and left me to kick as best I might in very deep water. I read the note over and over again; and for all my dilemma, I could not help laughing at the mingled meanness and stupidity of the thing. The picture of the host and hostess busying themselves in gumming together the torn letters of their departed guest struck me as one of the funniest things I could remember. And there was the stupidity of it, because surely a child could have seen that my mother's attack was in answer to my defence. Why should we write a duet each saying the same thing? Well, I'm still very confused about it all, and I don't in the least know what I am going to do - more likely to die on the last plank, than to get into port with my ensign mast-high. I must think it out and let you know the result. Come what may, one thing only is sure, and that is that, in weal or woe, I remain, ever, your affectionate and garrulous friend.

XIII.

1 OAKLEY VILLAS, BIRCHESPOOL,
12th June, 1882.

When I wrote my last letter, my dear Bertie, I was still gasping, like a cod on a sand-bank, after my final dismissal by Cullingworth. The mere setting of it all down in black and white seemed to clear the matter up, and I felt much more cheery by the time I had finished my letter. I was just addressing the envelope (observe what a continuous narrative you get of my proceedings!) when I was set jumping out of my carpet slippers by a ring at the bell. Through the glass panel I observed that it was a respectable-looking bearded individual with a top-hat. It was a patient. It MUST be a patient! Then first I realised what an entirely different thing it is to treat the patient of another man (as I had done with Horton) or to work a branch of another man's practice (as I had done with Cullingworth), and to have to do with a complete stranger on your own account. I had been thrilling to have one. Now that he had come I felt for an instant as if I would not open the door. But of course that was only a momentary weakness. I answered his ring with, I fear, rather a hypocritical air of insouciance, as though I had happened to find myself in the hall, and did not care to trouble the maid to ascend the stairs.

"Dr. Stark Munro?" he asked.

"Pray step in," I answered, and waved him into the consulting-room. He was a pompous, heavy-stepping, thick-voiced sort of person, but to me he was an angel from on high. I was nervous, and at the same time so afraid that he should detect my nervousness and lose confidence in me, that I found myself drifting into an extravagant geniality. He seated himself at my invitation and gave a husky cough.

"Ah," said I - I always prided myself on being quick at diagnosis - "bronchial, I perceive. These summer colds are a little trying."

"Yes," said he. "I've had it some time."

With a little care and treatment -- "I suggested.

He did not seem sanguine, but groaned and shook his head. "It's not about that I've come," said he.

"No?" My heart turned to lead.

"No, doctor." He took out a bulging notebook. "It's about a small sum that's due on the meter."

You'll laugh, Bertie, but it was no laughing matter to me. He wanted eight and sixpence on account of something that the last tenant either had or had not done. Otherwise the company would remove the gas-meter. How little he could have guessed that the alternative he was presenting to me was either to pay away more than half my capital, or to give up cooking my food! I at last appeased him by a promise that I should look into the matter, and so escaped for the moment, badly shaken but still solvent. He gave me a good deal of information about the state of his tubes (his own, not the gas company's) before he departed; but I had rather lost interest in the subject since I had learned that he was being treated by his club doctor.

That was the first of my morning incidents. My second followed hard upon the heels of it. Another ring came, and from my post of observation I saw that a gipsy's van, hung with baskets and wickerwork chairs, had drawn up at the door. Two or three people appeared to be standing outside. I understood that they wished me to purchase some of their wares, so I merely opened the door about three inches, said "No, thank you," and closed it. They seemed not to have heard me for they rang again, upon which I opened the door wider and spoke more decidedly. Imagine my surprise when they rang again. I flung the door open, and was about to ask them what they meant by their impudence, when one of the little group upon my doorstep said, "If you please, sir, it's the baby." Never was there such a change - from the outraged householder to the professional man. "Pray step in, madam," said I, in quite my most courtly style; and in they all came - the husband, the brother, the wife and the baby. The latter was in the early stage of measles. They were poor outcast sort of people, and seemed not to have sixpence among them; so my demands for a fee at the end of the consultation ended first in my giving the medicine for nothing, and finally adding fivepence in coppers, which was all the small change I had. A few more such patients and I am a broken man.

However, the two incidents together had the effect of taking up my attention and breaking the blow which I had had in the Cullingworth letter. It made me laugh to think that the apparent outsider should prove to be a patient, and the apparent patient an outsider. So back I went, in a much more judicial frame of mind, to read that precious document over again, and to make up my mind what it was that I should do.

And now I came to my first real insight into the depths which lie in the character of Cullingworth. I began by trying to recall how I could have torn up my mother's letters, for it is not usual for me to destroy papers in this manner. I have often been chaffed about the way in which I allow them to accumulate until my pockets become unbearable. The more I thought about it the more convinced I was that I could not have done anything of the sort; so finally I got out the little house jacket which I had usually worn at Bradfield, and I examined the sheaves of letters which it contained. It was there, Bertie! Almost the very first one that I opened was the identical one from which Cullingworth was quoting in which my mother had described him in those rather forcible terms.

Well, this made me sit down and gasp. I am, I think, one of the most unsuspicious men upon earth, and through a certain easy-going indolence of disposition I never even think of the possibility of those with whom I am brought in contact trying to deceive me. It does not occur to me. But let me once get on that line of thought - let me have proof that there is reason for suspicion - and then all faith slips completely away from me. Now I could see an explanation for much which had puzzled me at Bradfield. Those sudden fits of ill temper, the occasional ill-concealed animosity of Cullingworth - did they not mark the arrival of each of my mother's letters? I was convinced that they did. He had read them then - read them from the pockets of the little house coat which I used to leave carelessly in the hall when I put on my professional one to go out. I could remember, for example, how at the end of his illness his manner had suddenly changed on the very day when that final letter of my mother's had arrived. Yes, it was certain that he had read them from the beginning.

But a blacker depth of treachery lay beyond. If he had read them, and if he had been insane enough to think that I was acting disloyally towards him, why had he not said so at the time? Why had he contented himself with sidelong scowls and quarrelling over trivialities - breaking, too, into forced smiles when I had asked him point blank what was the matter? One obvious reason was that he could not tell his grievance without telling also how he had acquired his information. But I knew enough of Cullingworth's resource to feel that he could easily have got over such a difficulty as that. In fact, in this last letter he HAD got over it by his tale about the grate and the maid. He must have had some stronger reason for restraint. As I thought over the course of our relations I was convinced that his scheme was to lure me on by promises until I had committed myself, and then to abandon me, so that I should myself have no resource but to compound with my creditors-to be, in fact, that which my mother had called him.

But in that case he must have been planning it out almost from the beginning of my stay with him, for my mother's letters stigmatising his conduct had begun very early. For some time he had been uncertain how to proceed. Then he had invented the excuse (which seemed to me at the time, if you remember, to be quite inadequate) about the slight weekly decline in the practice in order to get me out of it. His next move was to persuade me to start for myself; and as this would be impossible without money, he had encouraged me to it by the promise of a small weekly loan. I remembered how he had told me not to be afraid about ordering furniture and other things, because tradesmen gave long credit to beginners, and I could always fall back upon him if necessary. He knew too from his own experience that the landlord would require at least a year's tenancy. Then he waited to spring his mine until I had written to say that I had finally committed myself, on which by return of post came his letter breaking the connection. It was so long and so elaborate a course of deceit, that I for the first time felt something like fear as I thought of Cullingworth. It was as though in the guise and dress of a man I had caught a sudden glimpse of something sub-human - of something so outside my own range of thought that I was powerless against it.

Well, I wrote him a little note - only a short one, but with, I hope, a bit of a barb to it. I said that his letter had been a source of gratification to me, as it removed the only cause for disagreement between my mother and myself. She had always thought him a blackguard, and I had always defended him; but I was forced now to confess that she had been right from the beginning. I said enough to show him that I saw through his whole plot; and I wound up by assuring him that if he thought he had done me any harm he had made a great mistake; for I had every reason to believe that he had unintentionally forced me into the very opening which I had most desired myself.

After this bit of bravado I felt better, and I thought over the situation. I was alone in a strange town, without connections, without introductions, with less than a pound in my pocket, and with no possibility of freeing myself from my responsibilities. I had no one at all to look to for help, for all my recent letters from home had given a dreary account of the state of things there. My poor father's health and his income were dwindling together. On the other hand, I reflected that there were some points in my favour. I was young. I was energetic. I had been brought up hard, and was quite prepared to rough it. I was well up in my work, and believed I could get on with patients. My house was an excellent one for my purpose, and I had already put the essentials of furniture into it. The game was not played out yet. I jumped to my feet and clenched my hand, and swore to the chandelier that it never should be played out until I had to beckon for help from the window.

For the next three days I had not a single ring at the bell of any sort whatever. A man could not be more isolated from his kind. It used to amuse me to sit upstairs and count how many of the passers-by stopped to look at my plate. Once (on a Sunday morning) there were over a hundred in an hour, and often I could see from their glancing over their shoulders as they walked on, that they were thinking or talking of the new doctor.

This used to cheer me up, and make me feel that something was going on.

Every night between nine and ten I slip out and do my modest shopping, having already made my MENU for the coming day. I come back usually with a loaf of bread, a paper of fried fish, or a bundle of saveloys. Then when I think things are sufficiently quiet, I go out and brush down the front with my broom, leaning it against the wall and looking up meditatively at the stars whenever anyone passes. Then, later still, I bring out my polishing paste, my rag, and my chamois leather; and I assure you that if practice went by the brilliancy of one's plate, I should sweep the town.

Who do you think was the first person who broke this spell of silence? The ruffian whom I had fought under the lamp-post. He is a scissors-grinder it seems, and rang to know if I had a job for him. I could not help grinning at him when I opened the door and saw who it was. He showed no sign of recognising me, however, which is hardly to be wondered at.

The next comer was a real bona fide patient, albeit a very modest one. She was a little anaemic old maid, a chronic hypochondriac I should judge, who had proba-bly worked her way round every doctor in the town, and was anxious to sample this novelty. I don't know whether I gave her satisfaction. She said that she would come again on Wednesday, but her eyes shifted as she said it. One and sixpence was as much as she could pay, but it was very welcome. I can live three days on one and sixpence.

I think that I have brought economy down to its finest point. No doubt, for a short spell I could manage to live on a couple of pence a day; but what I am doing now is not to be a mere spurt, but my regular mode of life for many a month to come. My tea and sugar and milk (Swiss) come collectively to one penny a day. The loaf is at twopence three-farthings, and I consume one a day. My dinner consists in rotation of one third of a pound of bacon, cooked over the gas (twopence halfpenny), or two saveloys (twopence), or two pieces of fried fish (twopence), or a quarter of an eightpenny tin of Chicago beef (twopence). Any one of these, with a due allowance of bread and water, makes a most substantial meal. Butter I have discarded for the present. My actual board therefore comes well under sixpence a day, but I am a patron of literature to the extent of a halfpenny a day, which I expend upon an evening paper; for with events hurrying on like this in Alexandria, I cannot bear to be without the news. Still I often reproach myself with that halfpenny, for if I went out in the evening and looked at the placards I might save it, and yet have a general idea of what is going on. Of course, a halfpenny a night sounds nothing, but think of a shilling a month! Perhaps you picture me as bloodless and pulled down on this diet! I am thin, it is true, but I never felt more fit in my life. So full of energy am I that I start off sometimes at ten at night and walk hard until two or three in the morning. I dare not go out during the day, you see, for fear that I should miss a patient. I have asked my mother not to send little Paul down yet until I see my way more clearly.

Old Whitehall came in to see me the other day. The object of his visit was to invite me to dinner, and the object of the dinner to inaugurate my starting in practice. If I were the kind old fellow's son he could not take a deeper interest in me and my prospects.

"By --, Dr. Munro, sir," said he, "I've asked every -- man in Birchespool that's got anything the matter with him. You'll have the lot as patients within a week. There's Fraser, who's got a touch of Martell's three star. He's coming. And there's Saunders, who talks about nothing but his spleen. I'm sick of his -- spleen! But I asked him. And there's Turpey's wound! This wet weather sets it tingling, and his own surgeon can do nothing but dab it with vaseline. He'll be there. And there's Carr, who is drinking himself to death. He has not much for the doctors, but what there is you may as well have."

All next day he kept popping in to ask me questions about the dinner. Should we have clear soup or ox-tail? Didn't I think that burgundy was better than port and sherry? The day after was the celebration itself, and he was in with a bulletin immediately after breakfast. The cooking was to be done at a neighbouring confectioner's. The landlady's son was coming in to wait. I was sorry to see that Whitehall was already slurring his words together, and had evidently been priming himself heavily. He looked in again in the afternoon to tell me what a good time we should have. So-and-so could talk well, and the other man could sing a song. He was so far gone by now, that I ventured (in the capacity of medical adviser) to speak to him about it.

It's not the liquor, Dr. Munro, sir," said he earnestly. It's the -- relaxing air of this town. But I'll go home and lie I'll down, and be as fresh as paint to welcome my guests."

But the excitement of the impending event must have been too much for him. When I arrived at five minutes to seven, Turpey, the wounded lieutenant, met me in the hall with a face of ill omen.

"It's all up with Whitehall," said he.

"What's the matter?"

"Blind, speechless and paralytic. Come and look."

The table in his room was nicely laid for dinner, and several decanters with a large cold tart lay upon the sideboard. On the sofa was stretched our unfortunate host, his head back, his forked beard pointing to the cornice, and a half finished tumbler of whisky upon the chair beside him. All our shakes and shouts could not break in upon that serene drunkenness.

"What are we to do?" gasped Turpey.

"We must not let him make an exhibition of himself. We had better get him away before any one else arrives."

So we bore him off, all in coils and curves like a dead python, and deposited him upon his bed. When we returned three other guests had arrived.

"You'll be sorry to hear that Whitehall is not very well," said Turpey. Dr. Munro thought it would be better that he should not come down."

"In fact, I have ordered him to bed," said I.

"Then I move that Mr. Turpey be called upon to act as host," said one of the new comers; and so it was at once agreed.

Presently the other men arrived; but there was no sign of the dinner. We waited for a quarter of an hour, but nothing appeared. The landlady was summoned, but could give no information.

"Captain Whitehall ordered it from a confectioner's, sir," said she, in reply to the lieutenant's cross-examination. "He did not tell me which confectioner's. It might have been any one of four or five. He only said that it would all come right, and that I should bake an apple tart."

Another quarter of an hour passed, and we were all ravenous. It was evident that Whitehall had made some mistake. We began to roll our eyes towards the apple pie, as the boat's crew does towards the boy in the stories of shipwreck. A large hairy man, with an anchor tattooed upon his hand, rose and set the pie in front of Turpey.

"What d'you say, gentlemen, - shall I serve it out?"

We all drew up at the table with a decision which made words superfluous. In five minutes the pie dish was as clean as when the cook first saw it. And our ill-luck vanished with the pie. A minute later the landlady's son entered with the soup; and cod's head, roast beef, game and ice pudding followed in due succession. It all came from some misunderstanding about time. But we did them justice, in spite of the curious hors d'oeuvre with which we had started; and a pleasanter dinner or a more enjoyable evening I have seldom had.

"Sorry I was so bowled over, Dr. Munro, sir," said Whitehall next morning. "I need hilly country and a bracing air, not a -- croquet lawn like this. Well, I'm -- glad to hear that you gentlemen enjoyed yourselves, and I hope you found everything to your satisfaction."

I assured him that we did; but I had not the heart to tell him about the apple pie.

I tell you these trivial matters, my dear Bertie, just to show you that I am not down on my luck, and that my life is not pitched in the minor key altogether, in spite of my queer situation. But, to turn to graver things: I was right glad to get your letter, and to read all your denunciations about dogmatic science. Don't imagine that my withers are wrung by what you say, for I agree with almost every word of it.

The man who claims that we can know nothing is, to my mind, as unreasonable as he who insists that everything has been divinely revealed to us. I know nothing more unbearable than the complacent type of scientist who knows very exactly all that he does know, but has not imagination enough to understand what a speck his little accumulation of doubtful erudition is when compared with the immensity of our ignorance. He is the person who thinks that the universe can be explained by laws, as if a law did not require construction as well as a world! The motion of the engine can be explained by the laws of physics, but that has not made the foregoing presence of an engineer less obvious. In this world, however, part of the beautiful poise of things depends upon the fact that whenever you have an exaggerated fanatic of any sort, his exact opposite at once springs up to neutralize him. You have a Mameluke: up jumps a Crusader. You have a Fenian: up jumps an Orangeman. Every force has its recoil. And so these more hide-bound scientists must be set against those gentlemen who still believe that the world was created in the year 4004 B. C.

After all, true science must be synonymous with religion, since science is the acquirement of fact; and facts are all that we have from which to deduce what we are and why we are here. But surely the more we pry into the methods by which results are brougt{sic} about, the more stupendous and wonderful becomes the great unseen power which lies behind, the power which drifts the solar system in safety through space, and yet adjusts the length of the insects proboscis to the depth of the honey-bearing flower. What is that central intelligence? You may fit up your dogmatic scientist with a 300-diameter microscope, and with a telescope with a six-foot speculum, but neither near nor far can he get a trace of that great driving power.

What should we say of a man who has a great and beautiful picture submitted to him, and who, having satisfied himself that the account given of the painting of the picture is incorrect, at once concludes that no one ever painted it, or at least asserts that he has no possible means of knowing whether an artist has produced it or not? That is, as it seems to me, a fair statement of the position of some of the more extreme agnostics. "Is not the mere existence of the picture in itself a proof that a skilful artist has been busied upon it? one might ask. "Why, no," says the objector. It is possible that the picture produced itself by the aid of certain rules. Besides, when the picture was first submitted to me I was assured that it had all been produced within a week, but by examining it I am able to say with certainty that it has taken a considerable time to put together. I am therefore of opinion that it is questionable whether any one ever painted it at all."

Leaving this exaggerated scientific caution on the one side, and faith on the other, as being equally indefensible, there remains the clear line of reasoning that a universe implies the existence of a universe maker, and that we may deduce from it some of His attributes, His power, His wisdom, His forethought for small wants, His providing of luxuries for His creatures. On the other hand, do not let us be disingenuous enough to shirk the mystery which lies in pain, in cruelty, in all which seems to be a slur upon

His work. The best that we can say for them is to hope that they are not as bad as they seem, and possibly lead to some higher end. The voices of the ill-used child and of the tortured animal are the hardest of all for the philosopher to answer.

Good-bye, old chap! It is quite delightful to think that on one point at least we are in agreement.

XIV.

1 OAKLEY VILLAS, BIRCHESPOOL,
15th January, 1883.

You write reproachfully, my dear Bertie, and you say that absence must have weakened our close friendship, since I have not sent you a line during this long seven months. The real truth of the matter is that I had not the heart to write to you until I could tell you something cheery; and something cheery has been terribly long in coming. At present I can only claim that the cloud has perhaps thinned a little at the edges.

You see by the address of this letter that I still hold my ground, but between ourselves it has been a terrible fight, and there have been times when that last plank of which old Whitehall wrote seemed to be slipping out of my clutch. I have ebbed and flowed, sometimes with a little money, sometimes without. At my best I was living hard, at my worst I was very close upon starvation. I have lived for a whole day upon the crust of a loaf, when I had ten pounds in silver in the drawer of my table. But those ten pounds had been most painfully scraped together for my quarter's rent, and I would have tried twenty-four hours with a tight leather belt before I would have broken in upon it. For two days I could not raise a stamp to send a letter. I have smiled when I have read in my evening paper of the privations of our fellows in Egypt. Their broken victuals would have been a banquet to me. However, what odds how you take your carbon and nitrogen and oxygen, as long as you DO get it? The garrison of Oakley Villa has passed the worst, and there is no talk of surrender.

It was not that I have had no patients. They have come in as well as could be expected. Some, like the little old maid, who was the first, never returned. I fancy that a doctor who opened his own door forfeited their confidence. Others have become warm partisans. But they have nearly all been very poor people; and when you consider how many one and sixpences are necessary in order to make up the fifteen pounds which I must find every quarter for rent, taxes, gas and water, you will understand that even with some success, I have still found it a hard matter to keep anything in the portmanteau which serves me as larder. However, my boy, two quarters are paid up, and I enter upon a third one with my courage unabated. I have lost about a stone, but not my heart.

I have rather a vague recollection of when it was exactly that my last was written. I fancy that it must have been a fortnight after my start, immediately after my breach with Cullingworth. It's rather hard to know where to begin when one has so many events to narrate, disconnected from each other, and trivial in themselves, yet which have each loomed large as I came upon them, though they look small enough now that they are so far astern. As I have mentioned Cullingworth, I may as well say first the little that is to be said about him. I answered his letter in the way which I have, I think, already described. I hardly expected to hear from him again; but my note had evidently stung him, and I had a brusque message in which he said that if I wished him to believe in my "bona-fides" (whatever he may have meant by that), I would return the money which I had had during the time that I was with him at Bradfield. To this I replied that the sum was about twelve pounds; that I still retained the message in which he had guaranteed me three hundred pounds if I came to Bradfield, that the balance in my favour was two hundred and eighty-eight pounds; and that unless I had a cheque by return, I should put the matter into the hands of my solicitor. This put a final end to our correspondence.

There was one other incident, however. One day after I had been in practice about two months, I observed a bearded commonplace-looking person lounging about on the other side of the road. In the afternoon he was again visible from my consulting-room window. When I saw him there once more next morning, my suspicions were aroused, and they became certainties when, a day or so afterwards, I came out of a patient's house in a poor street, and saw the same fellow looking into a greengrocer's shop upon the other side. I walked to the end of the street, waited round the corner, and met him as he came hurrying after.

"You can go back to Dr. Cullingworth, and tell him that I have as much to do as I care for," said I. "If you spy upon me after this it will be at your own risk."

He shuffled and coloured, but I walked on and saw him no more. There was no one on earth who could have had a motive for wanting to know exactly what I was doing except Cullingworth; and the man's silence was enough in itself to prove that I was right. I have heard nothing of Cullingworth since.

I had a letter from my uncle in the Artillery, Sir Alexander Munro, shortly after my start, telling me that he had heard of my proceedings from my mother, and that he hoped to learn of my success. He is, as I think you know, an ardent Wesleyan, like all my father's people, and he told me that the chief Wesleyan minister in the town was an old friend of his own, that he had learned from him that there was no Wesleyan doctor, and that, being of a Wesleyan stock myself, if I would present the enclosed letter of introduction to the minister, I should certainly find it very much to my advantage. I thought it over, Bertie, and it seemed to me that it would be playing it rather low down to use a religious organisation to my own advantage, when I condemned them in the abstract. It was a sore temptation, but I destroyed the letter.

I had one or two pieces of luck in the way of accidental cases. One (which was of immense importance to me) was that of a grocer named Haywood, who fell down in a fit outside the floor of his shop. I was passing on my way to see a poor labourer with typhoid. You may believe that I saw my chance, bustled in, treated the man, conciliated the wife, tickled the child, and gained over the whole household. He had these attacks periodically, and made an arrangement with me by which I was to deal with him, and we were to balance bills against each other. It was a ghoulish compact, by which a fit to him meant butter and bacon to me, while a spell of health for Haywood sent me back to dry bread and saveloys. However, it enabled me to put by for the rent many a shilling which must otherwise have gone in food. At last, however, the poor fellow died, and there was our final settlement.

Two small accidents occurred near my door (it was a

busy crossing), and though I got little enough from either of them, I ran down to the newspaper office on each occasion, and had the gratification of seeing in the evening edition that "the driver, though much shaken, is pronounced by Dr. Stark Munro, of Oakley Villa, to have suffered no serious injury." As Cullingworth used to say, it is hard enough for the young doctor to push his name into any publicity, and he must take what little chances he has. Perhaps the fathers of the profession would shake their heads over such a proceeding in a little provincial journal; but I was never able to see that any of them were very averse from seeing their own names appended to the bulletin of some sick statesman in The Times.

And then there came another and a more serious accident. This would be about two months after the beginning, though already I find it hard to put things in their due order. A lawyer in the town named Dickson was riding past my windows when the horse reared up and fell upon him. I was eating saveloys in the back room at the time, but I heard the noise and rushed to the door in time to meet the crowd who were carrying him in. They flooded into my house, thronged my hall, dirtied my consulting room, and even pushed their way into my back room, which they found elegantly furnished with a portmanteau, a lump of bread, and a cold sausage.

However, I had no thought for any one but my patient, who was groaning most dreadfully. I saw that his ribs were right, tested his joints, ran my hand down his limbs, and concluded that there was no break or dislocation. He had strained himself in such a way, however, that it was very painful to him to sit or to walk. I sent for an open carriage, therefore, and conveyed him to his home, I sitting with my most professional air, and he standing straight up between my hands. The carriage went at a walk, and the crowd trailed behind, with all the folk looking out of the windows, so that a more glorious advertisement could not be conceived. It looked like the advance guard of a circus. Once at his house, however, professional etiquette demanded that I should hand the case over to the family attendant, which I did with as good a grace as possible - not without some lingering hope that the old established practitioner might say, "You have taken such very good care of my patient, Dr. Munro, that I should not dream of removing him from your hands." On the contrary, he snatched it away from me with avidity, and I retired with some credit, an excellent advertisement, and a guinea.

These are one or two of the points of interest which show above the dead monotony of my life - small enough, as you see, but even a sandhill looms large in Holland. In the main, it is a dreary sordid record of shillings gained and shillings spent - of scraping for this and scraping for that, with ever some fresh slip of blue paper fluttering down upon me, left so jauntily by the tax-collector, and meaning such a dead-weight pull to me. The irony of my paying a poor-rate used to amuse me. I should have been collecting it. Thrice at a crisis I pawned my watch, and thrice I rallied and rescued it. But how am I to interest you in the details of such a career? Now, if a fair countess had been so good as to slip on a piece of orange peel before my door, or if the chief merchant in the town had been saved by some tour-de-force upon my part, or if I had been summoned out at midnight to attend some nameless person in a lonely house with a princely fee for silence - then I should have something worthy of your attention. But the long months and months during which I listened to the throb of the charwoman's heart and the rustle of the greengrocer's lungs, present little which is not dull and dreary. No good angels came my way.

Wait a bit, though! One did. I was awakened at six in the morning one day by a ringing at my bell, and creeping to the angle of the stair I saw through the glass a stout gentleman in a top-hat outside. Much excited, with a thousand guesses capping one another in my head, I ran back, pulled on some clothes, rushed down, opened the door, and found myself in the grey morning light face to face with Horton. The good fellow had come down from Merton in an excursion train, and had been travelling all night. He had an umbrella under his arm, and two great straw baskets in each hand, which contained, when unpacked, a cold leg of mutton, half-a-dozen of beer, a bottle of port, and all sorts of pasties and luxuries. We had a great day together, and when he rejoined his excursion in the evening he left a very much cheerier man than he had found.

Talking of cheeriness, you misunderstand me, Bertie, if you think (as you seem to imply) that I take a dark view of things. It is true that I discard some consolations which you possess, because I cannot convince myself that they are genuine; but in this world, at least, I see immense reason for hope, and as to the next I am confident that all will be for the best. From annihilation to beatification I am ready to adapt myself to whatever the great Designer's secret plan my be.

But there is much in the prospects of this world to set a man's heart singing. Good is rising and evil sinking like oil and water in a bottle. The race is improving. There are far fewer criminal convictions. There is far more education. People sin less and think more. When I meet a brutal looking fellow I often think that he and his type may soon be as extinct as the great auk. I am not sure that in the interest of the 'ologies we ought not to pickle a few specimens of Bill Sykes, to show our children's children what sort of a person he was.

And then the more we progress the more we tend to progress. We advance not in arithmetical but in geometrical progression. We draw compound interest on the whole capital of knowledge and virtue which has been accumulated since the dawning of time. Some eighty thousand years are supposed to have existed between paleolithic and neolithic man. Yet in all that time he only learned to grind his flint stones instead of chipping them. But within our father's lives what changes have there not been? The railway and the telegraph, chloroform and applied electricity. Ten years now go further than a thousand then, not so much on account of our finer intellects as because the light we have shows us the way to more. Primeval man stumbled along with peering eyes, and slow, uncertain footsteps. Now we walk briskly towards our unknown goal.

And I wonder what that goal is to be! I mean, of course, as far as this world is concerned. Ever since man first scratched hieroglyphics upon an ostracon, or scribbled with sepia upon papyrus, he must have wondered, as we wonder to-day. I suppose that we DO know a little more than they. We have an arc of about three thousand years given us, from which to calculate out the course to be described by our descendants; but that arc is so tiny when compared to the vast ages which Providence uses in working out its designs that our deductions from it must, I think, be uncertain. Will civilisation be swamped by barbarism? It happened once before, because the civilised were tiny specks of light in the midst of darkness. But what, for example, could break down the great country in which you dwell? No, our civilisation will endure and grow more complex. Man will live in the air and below the water. Preventive medicine will develop until old age shall become the sole cause of death. Education and a more socialistic scheme of society will do away with crime. The English-speaking races will unite, with their centre in the United States. Gradually the European States will follow their example. War will become rare, but more terrible. The forms of religion will be abandoned, but the essence will be maintained; so that one universal creed will embrace the whole civilised earth, which will preach trust in that central power, which will be as unknown then as now. That's my horoscope, and after that the solar system may be ripe for picking. But Bertie Swanborough and Stark Munro will be blowing about on the west wind, and dirtying the panes of careful housewives long before the half of it has come to pass.

And then man himself will change, of course. The teeth are going rapidly. You've only to count the dentists' brass plates in Birchespool to be sure of that. And the hair also. And the sight. Instinctively, when we think of the more advanced type of young man, we picture him as bald, and with double eye-glasses. I am an absolute animal myself, and my only sign of advance is that two of my back teeth are going. On the other hand, there is some evidence in favour of the development of a sixth sense-that of perception. If I had it now I should know that you are heartily weary of all my generalisations and dogmatism.

And certainly there must be a spice of dogmatism in it when we begin laying down laws about the future; for how do we know that there are not phases of nature coming upon us of which we have formed no conception? After all, a few seconds are a longer fraction of a day than an average life is of the period during which we know that the world has been in existence. But if a man lived only for a few seconds of daylight, his son the same, and his son the same, what would their united experiences after a hundred generations tell them of the phenomenon which we call night? So all our history and knowledge is no guarantee that our earth is not destined for experiences of which we can form no conception.

But to drop down from the universe to my own gnat's buzz of an existence, I think I have told you everything that might interest you of the first six months of my venture. Towards the end of that time my little brother Paul came down - and the best of companions he is! He shares the discomforts of my little menage in the cheeriest spirit, takes me out of my blacker humours, goes long walks with me, is interested in all that interests me (I always talk to him exactly as if he were of my own age), and is quite ready to turn his hand to anything, from boot-blacking to medicine-carrying. His one dissipation is cutting out of paper, or buying in lead (on the rare occasion when we find a surplus), an army of little soldiers. I have brought a patient into the consulting room, and found a torrent of cavalry, infantry, and artillery pouring across the table. I have been myself attacked as I sat silently writing, and have looked up to find fringes of sharp-shooters pushing up towards me, columns of infantry in reserve, a troop of

Sir A. C. Doyle

cavalry on my flank, while a battery of pea muzzle-loaders on the ridge of my medical dictionary has raked my whole position - with the round, smiling face of the general behind it all. I don't know how many regiments he has on a peace footing; but if serious trouble were to break out, I am convinced that every sheet of paper in the house would spring to arms.

One morning I had a great idea which has had the effect of revolutionising our domestic economy. It was at the time when the worst pinch was over, and when we had got back as far as butter and occasional tobacco, with a milkman calling daily; which gives you a great sense of swagger when you have not been used to it.

"Paul, my boy," said I, "I see my way to fitting up this house with a whole staff of servants for nothing."

He looked pleased, but not surprised. He had a wholly unwarranted confidence in my powers; so that if I had suddenly declared that I saw my way to tilting Queen Victoria from her throne and seating myself upon it, he would have come without a question to aid and abet.

I took a piece of paper and wrote, "To Let. A basement floor, in exchange for services. Apply 1 Oakley Villas."

"There, Paul," said I, "run down to the Evening News office, and pay a shilling for three insertions."

There was no need of three insertions. One would have been ample. Within half an hour of the appearance of the first edition, I had an applicant at the end of my bell-wire, and for the remainder of the evening Paul was ushering them in and I interviewing them with hardly a break. I should have been prepared at the outset to take anything in a petticoat; but as we saw the demand increase, our conditions went up and up; white aprons, proper dress for answering door, doing beds and boots, cooking, - we became more and more exacting. So at last we made our selection; a Miss Wotton, who asked leave to bring her sister with her. She was a hard-faced brusque-mannered person, whose appearance in a bachelor's household was not likely to cause a scandal. Her nose was in itself a certificate of virtue. She was to bring her furniture into the basement, and I was to give her and her sister one of the two upper rooms for a bedroom.

They moved in a few days later. I was out at the time, and the first intimation I had was finding three little dogs in my hall when I returned. I had her up, and explained that this was a breach of contract, and that I had no thoughts of running a menagerie. She pleaded very hard for her little dogs, which it seems are a mother and two daughters of some rare breed; so I at last gave in on the point. The other sister appeared to lead a subterranean troglodytic sort of existence; for, though I caught a glimpse of her whisking round the corner at times, it was a good month before I could have sworn to her in a police court.

For a time the arrangement worked well, and then there came complications. One morning, coming down earlier than usual, I saw a small bearded man undoing he inside chain of my door. I captured him before he could get it open. "Well," said I, "what's this?"

"If you please, sir," said he, "I'm Miss Wotton's husband."

Sir A. C. Doyle

Dreadful doubts of my housekeeper flashed across my mind, but I thought of her nose and was reassured. An examination revealed everything. She was a married woman. The lines were solemnly produced. Her husband was a seaman. She had passed as a miss, because she thought I was more likely to take a housekeeper without encumbrances. Her husband had come home unexpectedly from a long voyage, and had returned last night. And then - plot within plot - the other woman was not her sister, but a friend, whose name was Miss Williams. She thought I was more likely to take two sisters than two friends. So we all came to know who the other was; and I, having given Jack permission to remain, assigned the other top room to Miss Williams. From absolute solitude I seemed to be rapidly developing into the keeper of a casual ward.

It was a never-failing source of joy to us to see the procession pass on the way to their rooms at night. First came a dog; then Miss Williams, with a candle; then Jack; then another dog; and finally, Mrs. Wotton, with her candle in one hand and another dog under her arm. Jack was with us for three weeks; and as I made him holystone the whole place down twice a week until the boards were like a quarter deck, we got something out of him in return for his lodging.

About this time, finding a few shillings over and no expense imminent, I laid down a cellar, in the shape of a four and a half gallon cask of beer, with a firm resolution that it should never be touched save on high days and holidays, or when guests had to be entertained.

Shortly afterwards Jack went away to sea again; and after his departure there were several furious quarrels between the women down below, which filled the whole house with treble reproaches and repartees. At last one evening Miss Williams - the quiet one - came to me and announced with sobs that she must go. Mrs. Wotton made her life unbearable, she said. She was determined to be independent, and had fitted up a small shop in a poor quarter of the town. She was going now, at once, to take possession of it.

I was sorry, because I liked Miss Williams, and I said a few words to that effect. She got as far as the hall door, and then came rustling back again into the consulting room. "Take a drink of your own beer!" she cried, and vanished.

It sounded like some sort of slang imprecation. If she had said "Oh, pull up your socks!" I should have been less surprised. And then suddenly the words took a dreadful meaning in my mind, and I rushed to the cellar. The cask was tilted forward on the trestles. I struck it and it boomed like a drum. I turned the tap, and not one drop appeared. Let us draw a veil over the painful scene. Suffice it that Mrs. Wotton got her marching orders then and there - and that next day Paul and I found ourselves alone in the empty house once more.

But we were demoralised by luxury. We could no longer manage without a helper - especially now in the winter time, when fires had to be lit - the most heart-breaking task that a man can undertake. I bethought me of the quiet Miss Williams, and hunted her up in her shop. She was quite willing to come, and saw how she could get out of the rent; but the difficulty lay with her stock. This sounded formidable at first, but when I came to learn that the whole thing had cost eleven shillings, it did not appear insurmountable. In half an hour my watch was pawned, and the affair concluded. I returned with an excellent housekeeper, and with a larger basketful of inferior Swedish matches, boot-laces, cakes of black lead, and little figures made of sugar than I should have thought it possible to get for the money. So now we have settled down, and I hope that a period of comparative peace lies before us.

Good-bye, old chap, and never think that I forget you. Your letters are read and re-read with avidity. I think I have every line you ever wrote me. You simply knock Paley out every time. I am so glad that you got out of that brewery business all right. For a time I was really afraid that you must either lose your money or else risk more upon the shares. I can only thank you for your kind offer of blank cheques.

It is wonderful that you should have slipped back into your American life so easily after your English hiatus. As you say, however, it is not a change but only a modification, since the root idea is the same in each. Is it not strange how the two great brothers are led to misunderstand each other? A man is punished for private libel (over here at any rate), although the consequences can only be slight. But a man may perpetrate international libel, which is a very heinous and far-reaching offence, and there is no law in the world which can punish him. Think of the contemp-tible crew of journalists and satirists who for ever picture the Englishman as haughty and h-dropping, or the American as vulgar and expectorating. If some millionaire would give them all a trip round the world we should have some rest - and if the plug came out of the boat midway it would be more restful still. And your vote-hunting politicians with their tail-twisting campaigns, and our editors of the supercilious weeklies with their inane tone of superiority, if they were all aboard how much clearer we should be! Once more adieu, and good luck!

XV.

1 OAKLEY VILLAS, BIRCHESPOOL,
3rd August, 1883.

Do you think that such a thing as chance exists? Rather an explosive sentence to start a letter with; but pray cast your mind back over your own life, and tell me if you think that we really are the sports of chance. You know how often the turning down this street or that, the accepting or rejecting of an invitation, may deflect the whole current of our lives into some other channel. Are we mere leaves, fluttered hither and thither by the wind, or are we rather, with every conviction that we are free agents, carried steadily along to a definite and pre-determined end? I confess that as I advance through life, I become more and more confirmed in that fatalism to which I have always had an inclination.

Look at it in this way. We know that many of the permanent facts of the universe are NOT chance. It is not chance that the heavenly bodies swing clear of each other, that the seed is furnished with the apparatus which will drift it to a congenial soil, that the creature is adapted to its environment. Show me a whale with its great-coat of fat, and I want no further proof of design. But logically, as it seems to me, ALL must be design, or all must be chance. I do not see how one can slash a line right across the universe, and say that all to the right of that is chance, and all to the left is pre-ordained. You would then have to contend that things which on the face of them are of the same class, are really divided by an impassable gulf, and that the lower are regulated, while the higher are not. You would, for example, be forced to contend that the number of articulations in a flea's hind leg has engaged the direct superintendence of the Creator, while the mischance which killed a thousand people in a theatre depended upon the dropping of a wax vesta upon the floor, and was an unforeseen flaw in the chain of life. This seems to me to be unthinkable.

It is a very superficial argument to say that if a man holds the views of a fatalist he will therefore cease to strive, and will wait resignedly for what fate may send him. The objector forgets that among the other things fated is that we of northern blood SHOULD strive and should NOT sit down with folded hands. But when a man has striven, when he has done all he knows, and when, in spite of it, a thing comes to pass, let him wait ten years before he says that it is a misfortune. It is part of the main line of his destiny then, and is working to an end. A man loses his fortune; he gains earnestness. His eyesight goes; it leads him to a spirituality. The girl loses her beauty; she becomes more sympathetic. We think we are pushing our own way bravely, but there is a great Hand in ours all the time.

You'll wonder what has taken me off on this line. Only that I seem to see it all in action in my own life. But, as usual, I have started merrily off with an appendix, so I shall go back and begin my report as nearly as possible where I ended the last. First of all, I may say generally that the clouds were thinning then, and that they broke shortly afterwards. During the last few months we have never once quite lost sight of the sun.

You remember that we (Paul and I) had just engaged a certain Miss Williams to come and keep house for us. I felt that on the basement-lodger principle I had not control enough; so we now entered upon a more business-like arrangement, by which a sum (though, alas! An absurdly small one) was to be paid her for her services. I would it had been ten times as much, for a better and a more loyal servant man never had. Our fortunes seemed to turn from the hour that she re-entered the house.

Slowly, week by week, and month by month, the practice began to spread and to strengthen. There were spells when never a ring came to the bell, and it seemed as though all our labour had gone for nothing - but then would come other days when eight and ten names would appear in my ledger. Where did it come from you will ask. Some from old Whitehall and his circle of Bohemians. Some from accident cases. Some from new comers to the town who drifted to me. Some from people whom I met first in other capacities. An insurance superintendent gave me a few cases to examine, and that was a very great help. Above all, I learned a fact which I would whisper in the ear of every other man who starts, as I have done, a stranger among strangers. Do not think that practice will come to you. You must go to it. You may sit upon your consulting room chair until it breaks under you, but without purchase or partnership you will make little or no progress. The way to do it is to go out, to mix everywhere with men, to let them know you. You will come back many a time and be told by a reproachful housekeeper that some one has been for you in your absence. Never mind! Go out again. A noisy smoking concert where you will meet eighty men is better for you than the patient or two whom you might have seen at home. It took me some time to realise, but I speak now as one who knows.

But - there is a great big "but" in the case. You must ride yourself on the curb the whole time. Unless you re sure - absolutely sure - that you can do this, you are far best at home. You must never for one instant forget yourself. You must remember what your object is in being there. You must inspire respect. Be friendly, genial, convivial - what you will - but preserve the tone and bearing of a gentleman. If you can make yourself respected and liked you will find every club and society that you join a fresh introduction to practice. But beware of drink! Above everything, beware of drink! The company that you are in may condone it in each other, but never in the man who wishes them to commit their lives to his safe keeping. A slip is fatal - a half slip perilous. Make your rule of life and go by it, in spite of challenge or coaxers. It will be remembered in your favour next morning.

And of course I do not mean merely festive societies. Literary, debating, political, social, athletic, every one of them is a tool to your hands. But you must show them what a good man you are. You must throw yourself into each with energy and conviction. You will soon find yourself on the committee - possibly the secretary, or even in the presidential chair. Do not grudge labour where the return may be remote and indirect. Those are the rungs up which one climbs.

That was how, when I had gained some sort of opening, I set to work to enlarge it. I joined this. I joined that. I pushed in every direction. I took up athletics again much to the advantage of my health, and found that the practice benefited as well as I. My cricket form for the season has been fair, with an average of about 20 with the bat and 9 with the ball.

It must be allowed, however, that this system of sallying out for my patients and leaving my consulting room empty might be less successful if it were not for my treasure of a housekeeper. She is a marvel of discretion, and the way in which she perjures her soul for the sake of the practice is a constant weight upon my conscience. She is a tall, thin woman, with a grave face and an impressive manner. Her standard fiction, implied rather than said (with an air as if it were so universally known that it would be absurd to put it into words) is, that I am so pressed by the needs of my enormous practice, that any one wishing to consult me must make their appointment very exactly and a long time in advance.

"Dear me, now!" she says to some applicant. He's been hurried off again. If you'd been here half-an-hour ago he might have given you a minute. I never saw such a thing" (confidentially). "Between you and me I don't think he can last at it long. He's bound to break down. But come in, and I'll do all I can for you."

Then, having carefully fastened the patient up in the consulting room, she goes to little Paul.

"Run round to the bowling green, Master Paul," says she. "You'll find the doctor there, I think. Just tell him that a patient is waiting for him."

She seems in these interviews to inspire them with a

kind of hushed feeling of awe, as if they had found their way into some holy of holies. My own actual appearance is quite an anti-climax after the introduction by Miss Williams.

Another of her devices is to make appointments with an extreme precision as to time, I being at the moment worked to death (at a cricket match).

"Let us see!" says she, looking at the slate. "He will be clear at seven minutes past eight this evening. Yes, he could just manage it then. He has no one at all from seven past to the quarter past" - and so at the appointed hour I have my patient precipitating himself into my room with the demeanour of the man who charges in for his bowl of hot soup at a railway station. If he knew that he is probably the only patient who has opened my door that evening he would not be in such a hurry - or think so much of my advice.

One curious patient has come my way who has been of great service to me. She is a stately looking widow, Turner by name, the most depressingly respectable figure, as of Mrs. Grundy's older and less frivolous sister. She lives in a tiny house, with one small servant to scale. Well, every two months or so she quite suddenly goes on a mad drink, which lasts for about a week. It ends as abruptly as it begins, but while it is on the neighbours know it. She shrieks, yells, sings, chivies the servant, and skims plates out of the window at the passers-by. Of course, it is really not funny, but pathetic and deplorable - all the same, it is hard to keep from laughing at the absurd contrast between her actions and her appearance. I was called in by accident in the first instance; but I speedily acquired some control over her, so that now the neighbours send for me the moment the crockery begins to come through the window. She has a fair competence, so that her little vagaries are a help to me with my rent. She has, too, a number of curious jugs, statues, and pictures, a selection of which she presents to me in the course of each of her attacks, insisting upon my carrying them away then and there; so that I stagger out of the house like one of Napoleon's generals coming out of Italy. There is a good deal of method in the old lady, however, and on her recovery she invariably sends round a porter, with a polite note to say that she would be very glad to have her pictures back again.

And now I have worked my way to the point where I can show you what I mean when I talk about fate. The medical practitioner who lives next me - Porter is his name - is a kindly sort of man, and knowing that I have had a long uphill fight, he has several times put things in my way. One day about three weeks ago he came into my consulting room after breakfast.

"Could you come with me. to a consultation?" he asked.

"With pleasure."

"I have my carriage outside."

He told me something of the case as we went. It was a young fellow, an only son, who had been suffering from nervous symptoms for some time, and lately from considerable pain in his head. "His people are living with a patient of mine, General Wainwright," said Porter. "He didn't like the symptoms, and thought he would have a second opinion."

We came to the house, a great big one, in its own grounds, and had a preliminary talk with the dark-faced, white-haired Indian soldier who owns it. He was explaining the responsibility that he felt, the patient being his nephew, when a lady entered the room. "This is my sister, Mrs. La Force," said he, "the mother of the gentleman whom you are going to see."

I recognised her instantly. I had met her before and under curious circumstances. (Dr. Stark Munro here proceeds to narrate again how he had met the La Forces, having evidently forgotten that he had already done so in Letter VI.) When she was introduced I could see that she had not associated me with the young doctor in the train. I don't wonder, for I have started a beard, in the hope of making myself look a little older. She was naturally all anxiety about her son, and we went up with her (Porter and I) to have a look at him. Poor fellow! he seemed peakier and more sallow than when I had seen him last. We held our consultation, came to an agreement about the chronic nature of his complaint, and finally departed without my reminding Mrs. La Force of our previous meeting.

Well, there the matter might have ended; but about three days afterwards who should be shown into my consulting room but Mrs. La Force and her daughter. I thought the latter looked twice at me, when her mother introduced her, as if she had some recollection of my face; but she evidently could not recall where she had seen it, and I said nothing to help her. They both seemed to be much distressed in mind - indeed, the tears were brimming over from the girl's eyes, and her lip was quivering.

"We have come to you, Doctor Munro, in the greatest

distress," said Mrs. La Force; "we should be very glad of your advice."

"You place me in rather a difficult position, Mrs. La Force," said I. "The fact is, that I look upon you as Dr. Porter's patients, and it is a breach of etiquette upon my part to hold any communication with you except through him."

"It was he who sent us here," said she.

"Oh, that alters the matter entirely."

"He said he could do nothing to help us, and that perhaps you could."

"Pray let me know what you wish done."

She set out valorously to explain; but the effort of putting her troubles into words seemed to bring them more home to her, and she suddenly blurred over and became inarticulate. Her daughter bent towards her, and kissed her with the prettiest little spasm of love and pity.

"I will tell you about it, doctor," said she. "Poor mother is almost worn out. Fred - my brother, that is to say, is worse. He has become noisy, and will not be quiet."

"And my brother, the general," continued Mrs. La Force, "naturally did not expect this when he kindly offered us a home, and, being a nervous man, it is very trying to him. In fact, it cannot go on. He says so himself."

"But what is mother to do?" cried the girl, taking up

the tale again. "No hotel or lodging-house would take us in while poor Fred is like that. And we have not the heart to send him to an asylum. Uncle will not have us any longer, and we have nowhere to go to." Her grey eyes tried to look brave, but her mouth would go down at the corners.

I rose and walked up and down the room, trying to think it all out.

"What I wanted to ask you," said Mrs. La Force, "was whether perhaps you knew some doctor or some private establishment which took in such cases - so that we could see Fred every day or so. The only thing is that he must be taken at once, for really my brother has reached the end of his patience."

I rang the bell for my housekeeper.

"Miss Williams," said I, "do you think we can furnish a bedroom by to-night, so as to take in a gentleman who is ill?"

Never have I so admired that wonderful woman's self-command.

"Why, easily, sir, if the patients will only let me alone. But with that bell going thirty times an hour, it's hard to say what you are going to do."

This with her funny manner set the ladies laughing, and the whole business seemed lighter and easier. I promised to have the room ready by eight o'clock. Mrs. La Force arranged to bring her son round at that hour, and both ladies thanked me a very great deal more than I deserved; for after all it was a business matter, and a resident patient was the very thing that I needed. I was able to assure Mrs. La Force that I had had a similar case under my charge before - meaning, of course, poor "Jimmy," the son of Lord Saltire. Miss Williams escorted them to the door, and took occasion to whisper to them that it was wonderful how I got through with it, and that I was within sight of my carriage."

It was a short notice, but we got everything ready by the hour. Carpet, bed, suite, curtains - all came together, and were fixed in their places by the united efforts of Miss Williams, Paul, and myself. Sharp at eight a cab arrived, and Fred was conducted by me into his bedroom. The moment I looked at him I could see that he was much worse than when I saw him with Dr. Porter. The chronic brain trouble had taken a sudden acute turn.

His eyes were wild, his cheeks flushed, his lips drawn slightly away from his teeth. His temperature was 102@, and he muttered to himself continually, and paid no attention to my questions. It was evident to me at a glance that the responsibility which I had taken upon myself was to be no light one.

However, we could but do our best. I undressed him and got him safely to bed, while Miss Williams prepared some arrowroot for his supper. He would eat nothing, however, but seemed more disposed to dose, so having seen him settle down we left him. His room was the one next to mine, and as the wall was thin, I could hear the least movement. Two or three times he muttered and groaned, but finally he became quiet, and I was able to drop to sleep.

At three in the morning, I was awakened by a dreadful crash. Bounding out of bed I rushed into the other room. Poor Fred was standing in his long gown, a pathetic little figure in the grey light of the dawning day. He had pulled over his washing-stand (with what object only his bemuddled mind could say), and the whole place was a morass of water with islands of broken crockery. I picked him up and put him back into his bed again - his body glowing through his night-dress, and his eyes staring wildly about him. It was evidently impossible to leave him, and so I spent the rest of the night nodding and shivering in the armchair. No, it was certainly not a sinecure that I had undertaken.

In the morning I went round to Mrs. La Force and gave her a bulletin. Her brother had recovered his serenity now that the patient had left. He had the Victoria Cross it seems, and was one of the desperate little garrison who held Lucknow in that hell-whirl of a mutiny. And now the sudden opening of a door sets him shaking, and a dropped tongs gives him palpitations. Are we not the strangest kind of beings?

Fred was a little better during the day, and even seemed in a dull sort of way to recognise his sister, who brought him flowers in the afternoon. Towards evening his temperature sank to 101.5@, and he fell into a kind of stupor. As it happened, Dr. Porter came in about supper-time, and I asked him if he would step up and have a look at my patient. He did so, and we found him dozing peacefully. You would hardly think that that small incident may have been one of the most momentous in my life. It was the merest chance in the world that Porter went up at all.

Sir A. C. Doyle

Fred was taking medicine with a little chloral in it at this time. I gave him his usual dose last thing at night; and then, as he seemed to be sleeping peacefully, I went to my own room for the rest which I badly needed. I did not wake until eight in the morning, when I was roused by the jingling of a spoon in a saucer, and the step of Miss Williams passing my door. She was taking him the arrowroot which I had ordered over-night. I heard her open the door, and the next moment my heart sprang into my mouth as she gave a hoarse scream, and her cup and saucer crashed upon the floor. An instant later she had burst into my room, with her face convulsed with terror.

"My God!" she cried, "he's gone!"

I caught up my dressing-gown and rushed into the next room.

Poor little Fred was stretched sideways across his bed, quite dead. He looked as if he had been rising and had fallen backwards. His face was so peaceful and smiling that I could hardly have recognised the worried, fever-worn features of yesterday. There is great promise, I think, on the faces of the dead. They say it is but the post-mortem relaxation of the muscles, but it is one of the points on which I should like to see science wrong.

Miss Williams and I stood for five minutes without a word, hushed by the presence of that supreme fact. Then we laid him straight, and drew the sheet over him. She knelt down and prayed and sobbed, while I sat on the bed, with the cold hand in mine. Then my heart turned to lead as I remembered that it lay for me to break the news to the mother.

However, she took it most admirably. They were all three at breakfast when I came round, the general, Mrs. La Force, and the daughter. Somehow they seemed to know all that I had to say at the very sight of me; and in their womanly unselfishness their sympathy was all for me, for the shock I had suffered, and the disturbance of my household. I found myself turned from the consoler into the consoled. For an hour or more we talked it over, I explaining what I hope needed no explanation, that as the poor boy could not tell me his symptoms it was hard for me to know how immediate was his danger. There can be no doubt that the fall of temperature and the quietness which both Porter and I had looked upon as a hopeful sign, were really the beginning to the end.

Mrs. La Force asked me to see to everything, the formalities, register, and funeral. It was on a Wednesday, and we thought it best that the burial should be on the Friday. Back I hurried, therefore, not knowing what to do first, and found old Whitehall waiting for me in my consulting room, looking very jaunty with a camellia in his button-hole. Not an organ in its right place, and a camelia in his button-hole!

Between ourselves, I was sorry to see him, for I was in no humour for his company; but he had heard all about it from Miss Williams, and had come to stop. Only then did I fully realise how much of the kindly, delicate-minded gentleman remained behind that veil of profanity and obscenity which he so often held before him.

"I'll trot along with you, Dr. Munro, sir. A man's none the worse for a companion at such times. I'll not open my mouth unless you wish it, sir; but I am an idle man, and would take it as a kindness if you would let me come round with you."

Round he came, and very helpful he was. He seemed to know all about the procedure - "Buried two wives, Dr. Munro, sir! "I signed the certificate myself, conveyed it to the registrar, got the order for burial, took it round to the parish clerk, arranged an hour, then off to the undertaker's, and back to my practice. It was a kind of nightmare morning to look back upon, relieved only by the figure of my old Bohemian, with his pea jacket, his black thorn, his puffy, crinkly face, and his camelia.

To make a long story short, then, the funeral came off as arranged, General Wainwright, Whitehall, and I being the sole mourners. The captain had never seen poor Fred in the flesh, but he "liked to be in at the finish, sir," and so he gave me his company. It was at eight in the morning, and it was ten before we found ourselves at Oakley Villa. A burly man with bushy whiskers was waiting for us at the door.

"Are you Dr. Munro, sir?" he asked.

"I am."

"I am a detective from the local office. I was ordered to inquire into the death of the young man in your house lately."

Here was a thunderbolt! If looking upset is a sign of guilt, I must have stood confessed as a villain. It was so absolutely unexpected. I hope, however, that I had command of myself instantly.

"Pray step in!" said I. Any information I can give you is entirely at your service. Have you any objection to my friend Captain Whitehall being present?

"Not in the least." So in we both went, taking this bird of ill-omen.

He was, however, a man of tact and with a pleasant manner.

"Of course, Dr. Munro," said he, "you are much too well known in the town for any one to take this matter seriously. But the fact is that we had an anonymous letter this morning saying that the young man had died yesterday and was to be buried at an unusual hour to-day, and that the circumstances were suspicious."

He died the day before yesterday. He was buried at eight to-day," I explained; and then I told him the hole story from the beginning. He listened attentively and took a note or two.

"Who signed the certificate?" he asked.

"I did," said I.

He raised his eyebrows slightly. "There is really no one to check your statement then?" said he.

"Oh yes, Dr. Porter saw him the night before he died. He knew all about the case."

The detective shut his note-book with a snap. "That is final, Dr. Munro," said he. "Of course I must see Dr. Porter as a matter of form, but if his opinion agrees with yours I can only apologise to you for this intrusion."

"And there is one more thing, Mr. Detective, sir," said Whitehall explosively. "I'm not a rich man, sir, only the -- half-pay skipper of an armed transport; but by --, sir, I'd give you this hat full of dollars to know the name of the -- rascal who wrote that anonymous letter, sir. By -- sir, you'd have a real case to look after then." And he waved his black thorn ferociously.

So the wretched business ended, Bertie. But on what trifling chances do our fortunes depend! If Porter had not seen him that night, it is more than likely that there would have been an exhumation. And then, - well, there would be chloral in the body; some money interests DID depend upon the death of the lad - a sharp lawyer might have made much of the case. Anyway, the first breath of suspicion would have blown my little rising practice to wind. What awful things lurk at the corners of Life's highway, ready to pounce upon us as we pass!

And so you really are going a-voyaging! Well, I won't write again until I hear that you are back from the Islands, and then I hope to have something a little more cheery to talk about.

XVI.

1 OAKLEY VILLAS, BIRCHESPOOL,
4th November, 1884.

I face my study window as I write, Bertie. Slate-coloured clouds with ragged fringes are drifting slowly overhead. Between them one has a glimpse of higher clouds of a lighter gray. I can hear the gentle swish of the rain striking a clearer note on the gravel path and a duller among the leaves. Sometimes it falls straight and heavy, till the air is full of the delicate gray shading, and for half a foot above the ground there is a haze from the rebound of a million tiny globules. Then without any change in the clouds it cases off again. Pools line my walk, and lie thick upon the roadway, their surface pocked by the falling drops. As I sit I can smell the heavy perfume of the wet earth, and the laurel bushes gleam where the light strikes sideways upon them. The gate outside shines above as though it were new varnished, and along the lower edge of the upper bar there hangs a fringe of great clear drops.

That is the best that November can do for us in our dripping little island. You, I suppose, sitting among the dying glories of an American fall, think that this must needs be depressing. Don't make any mistake about that, my dear boy. You may take the States, from Detroit to the Gulf, and you won't find a happier man than this one. What do you suppose I've got att his{sic

- at this} moment in my consulting room? A bureau? A bookcase? No, I know you've guessed my secret already. She is sitting in my big armchair; and she is the best, the kindest, the sweetest little woman in England.

Yes, I've been married six months now - the almanack says months, though I should have thought weeks. I should, of course, have sent cake and cards, but had an idea that you were not home from the Islands yet. It is a good year since I wrote to you; but when you give an amorphous address of that sort, what can you expect? I've thought of you, and talked of you often enough.

Well, I daresay, with the acumen of an old married man, you have guessed who the lady is as well. We surely know by some nameless instinct more about our futures than we think we know. I can remember, for example, that years ago the name of Bradfield used to strike with a causeless familiarity upon my ear; and since then, as you know, the course of my life has flowed through it. And so when I first saw Winnie La Force in the railway carriage, before I had spoken to her or knew her name, I felt an inexplicable sympathy for and interest in her. Have you had no experience of the sort in your life? Or was it merely that she was obviously gentle and retiring, and so made a silent claim upon all that was helpful and manly in me? At any rate, I was conscious of it; and again and again every time that I met her. How good is that saying of some Russian writer that he who loves one woman knows more of the whole sex than he who has had passing relations with a thousand! I thought I knew something of women. I suppose every medical student does. But now I can see that I really knew nothing. My knowledge was all external. I did not know the woman soul, that crowning gift of Providence to man, which, if we do not ourselves degrade it, will set an edge to all that is good in us. I did not know how the love of a woman will tinge a man's whole life and every action with unselfishness. I did not know how easy it is to be noble when some one else takes it for granted that one will be so; or how wide and interesting life becomes when viewed by four eyes instead of two. I had much to learn, you see; but I think I have learned it.

It was natural that the death of poor Fred La Force should make me intimate with the family. It was really that cold hand which I grasped that morning as I sat by his bed which drew me towards my happiness. I visited them frequently, and we often went little excursions together. Then my dear mother came down to stay with me for a spell, and turned Miss Williams gray by looking for dust in all sorts of improbable corners; or advancing with a terrible silence, a broom in one hand and a shovel in the other, to the attack of a spider's web which she had marked down in the beer cellar. Her presence enabled me to return some of the hospitality which I had received from the La Forces, and brought us still nearer together.

I had never yet reminded them of our previous meeting. One evening, however, the talk turned upon clairvoyance, and Mrs. La Force was expressing the utmost disbelief in it. I borrowed her ring, and holding it to my forehead, I pretended to be peering into her past.

"I see you in a railway carriage," said I. "You are wearing a red feather in your bonnet. Miss La Force is dressed in something dark. There is a young man there. He is rude enough to address your daughter as Winnie before he has ever been -- "

"Oh, mother," she cried, "of course it is he! The face haunted me, and I could not think where we had met it."

Well, there are some things that we don't talk about to another man, even when we know each other as well as I know you. Why should we, when that which is most engrossing to us consists in those gradual shades of advance from friendship to intimacy, and from intimacy to something more sacred still, which can scarcely be written at all, far less made interesting to another? The time came at last when they were to leave Birchespool, and my mother and I went round the night before to say goodbye. Winnie and I were thrown together for an instant.

"When will you come back to Birchespool?" I asked.

"Mother does not know."

"Will you come soon, and be my wife?"

I had been turning over in my head all the evening how prettily I could lead up to it, and how neatly I could say it - and behold the melancholy result! Well, perhaps the feeling of my heart managed to make itself clear even through those bald words. There was but one to judge, and she was of that opinion.

I was so lost in my own thoughts that I walked as far as Oakley Villa with my mother before I opened my mouth. "Mam," said I at last, "I have proposed to Winnie La Force, and she has accepted me."

"My boy," said she, "you are a true Packenham." And so I knew that my mother's approval had reached the point of enthusiasm. It was not for days - not until I expressed a preference for dust under the bookcase with quiet, against purity and ructions - that the dear old lady perceived traces of the Munros.

The time originally fixed for the wedding was six months after this; but we gradually whittled it down to five and to four. My income had risen to about two hundred and seventy pounds at the time; and Winnie had agreed, with a somewhat enigmatical smile, that we could manage very well on that - the more so as marriage sends a doctor's income up. The reason of her smile became more apparent when a few weeks before that date I received a most portentous blue document in which "We, Brown & Woodhouse, the solicitors for the herein and hereafter mentioned Winifred La Force, do hereby" - state a surprising number of things, and use some remarkably bad English. The meaning of it, when all the "whereas's and aforesaids" were picked out, was, that Winnie had about a hundred a year of her own. It could not make me love her a shade better than I did; but at the same time I won't be so absurd as to say that I was not glad, or to deny that it made our marriage much easier than it would otherwise have been.

Poor Whitehall came in on the morning of the ceremony. He was staggering under the weight of a fine Japanese cabinet which he had carried round from his lodgings. I had asked him to come to the church, and the old gentleman was resplendent in a white waistcoat and a silk tie. Between ourselves, I had been just a little uneasy lest his excitement should upset him, as in the case of the dinner; but nothing could be more exemplary than his conduct and appearance. I had introduced him to Winnie some days before.

"You'll forgive me for saying, Dr. Munro, sir, that you are a -- lucky fellow," said he. "You've put your hand in the bag, sir, and taken out the eel first time, as any one with half an eye can see. Now, I've had three dips, and landed a snake every dip. If I'd had a good woman at my side, Dr. Munro, sir, I might not be the broken half-pay skipper of an armed transport to-day."

"I thought you had been twice married, captain."

"Three times, sir. I buried two. The other lives at Brussels. Well, I'll be at the church, Dr. Munro, sir; and you may lay that there is no one there who wishes you better than I do."

And yet there were many there who wished me well. My patients had all got wind of it; and they assembled by the pew-full, looking distressingly healthy. My neighbour, Dr. Porter, was there also to lend me his support, and old General Wainwright gave Winnie away. My mother, Mrs. La Force, and Miss Williams were all in the front pew; and away at the back of the church I caught a glimpse of the forked beard and crinkly face of Whitehall, and beside him the wounded lieutenant, the man who ran away with the cook, and quite a line of the strange Bohemians who followed his fortunes. Then when the words were said, and man's form had tried to sanctify that which was already divine, we walked amid the pealings of the "Wedding March" into the vestry, where my dear mother relieved the tension of the situation by signing the register in the wrong place, so that to all appearance it was she who had just married the clergyman. And then amid congratulations and kindly faces, we were together, her hand on my forearm, upon the steps of the church, and saw the familiar road stretching before us. But it was not that road which lay before my eyes, but rather the path of our lives; - that broader path on which our feet were now planted, so pleasant to tread, and yet with its course so shrouded in the mist. Was it long, or was it short? Was it uphill, or was it down? For her, at least, it should be smooth, if a man's love could make it so.

We were away for several weeks in the Isle of Man, and then came back to Oakley Villa, where Miss Williams was awaiting us in a house in which even my mother could have found no dust, and with a series of cheering legends as to the crowds of patients who had blocked the street in my absence. There really was a marked increase in my practice; and for the last six months or so, without being actually busy, I have always had enough to occupy me. My people are poor, and I have to work hard for a small fee; but I still study and attend the local hospital, and keep my knowledge up-to-date, so as to be ready for my opening when it comes. There are times when I chafe that I may not play a part upon some larger stage than this; but my happiness is complete, and if fate has no further use for me, I am content now from my heart to live and to die where I am.

You will wonder, perhaps, how we get on - my wife and I - in the matter of religion. Well, we both go our own ways. Why should I proselytise? I would not for the sake of abstract truth take away her child-like faith which serves to make life easier and brighter to her. I have made myself ill-understood by you in these discursive letters if you have read in them any bitterness against the orthodox creeds. Far from saying that they are all false, it would express my position better to say that they are all true. Providence would not have used them were they not the best available tools, and in that sense divine. That they are final I deny. A simpler and more universal creed will take their place, when the mind of man is ready for it; and I believe it will be a creed founded upon those lines of absolute and provable truth which I have indicated. But the old creeds are still the best suited to certain minds, and to certain ages. If they are good enough for Providence to use, they are good enough for us to endure. We have but to wait upon the survival of the truest. If I have seemed to say anything aggressive against them, it was directed at those who wish to limit the Almighty's favour to their own little clique, or who wish to build a Chinese wall round religion, with no assimilation of fresh truths, and no hope of expansion in the future. It is with these that the pioneers of progress can hold no truce. As for my wife, I would as soon think of breaking in upon her innocent prayers, as she would of carrying off the works of philosophy from my study table. She is not narrow in her views; but if one could stand upon the very topmost pinnacle of broad-mindedness, one would doubtless see from it that even the narrow have their mission.

About a year ago I had news of Cullingworth from Smeaton, who was in the same football team at college, and who had called when he was passing through Bradfield. His report was not a very favourable one. The practice had declined considerably. People had no doubt accustomed themselves to his eccentricities, and these had ceased to impress them. Again, there had been one or two coroner's inquests, which had spread the impression that he had been rash in the use of powerful drugs. If the coroner could have seen the hundreds of cures which Cullingworth had effected by that same rashness he would have been less confident with his censures. But, as you can understand, C.'s rival medical men were not disposed to cover him in any way. He had never had much consideration for them.

Besides this decline in his practice, I was sorry to hear that Cullingworth had shown renewed signs of that curious vein of suspicion which had always seemed to me to be the most insane of all his traits. His whole frame of mind towards me had been an example of it, but as far back as I can remember it had been a characteristic. Even in those early days when they lived in four little rooms above a grocer's shop, I recollect that he insisted upon gumming up every chink of one bedroom for fear of some imaginary infection. He was haunted, too, with a perpetual dread of eavesdroppers, which used to make him fly at the door and fling it open in the middle of his conversation, pouncing out into the passage with the idea of catching somebody in the act. Once it was the maid with the tea tray that he caught, I remember; and I can see her astonished face now, with an aureole of flying cups and lumps of sugar.

Smeaton tells me that this has now taken the form of imagining that some one is conspiring to poison him with copper, against which he takes the most extravagant precautions. It is the strangest sight, he says, to see Cullingworth at his meals; for he sits with an elaborate chemical apparatus and numerous retorts and bottles at his elbow, with which he tests samples of every course. I could not help laughing at Smeaton's description, and yet it was a laugh with a groan underlying it. Of all ruins, that of a fine man is the saddest.

I never thought I should have seen Cullingworth again, but fate has brought us together. I have always had a kindly feeling for him, though I feel that he used me atrociously. Often I have wondered whether, if I were placed before him, I should take him by the throat or by the hand. You will be interested to hear what actually occurred.

One day, just a week or so back, I was starting on my round, when a boy arrived with a note. It fairly took my breath away when I saw the familiar writing, and realised that Cullingworth was in Birchespool. I called Winnie, and we read it together.

"Dear Munro," it said, "James is in lodgings here for a few days. We are on the point of leaving England. He would be glad, for the sake of old times, to have a chat with you before he goes.

"Yours faithfully,

"HETTY CULLINGWORTH."

The writing was his and the style of address, so that it was evidently one of those queer little bits of transparent cunning which were characteristic of him, to make it come from his wife, that he might not lay himself open to a direct rebuff. The address, curiously enough, was that very Cadogan Terrace at which I had lodged, but two doors higher up.

Well, I was averse from going myself, but Winnie was all for peace and forgiveness. Women who claim nothing invariably get everything, and so my gentle little wife always carries her point. Half an hour later I was in Cadogan Terrace with very mixed feelings, but the kindlier ones at the top. I tried to think that Cullingworth's treatment of me had been pathological - the result of a diseased brain. If a delirious man had struck me, I should not have been angry with him. That must be my way of looking at it.

If Cullingworth still bore any resentment, he concealed it most admirably. But then I knew by experience that that genial loud-voiced John-Bull manner of his COULD conceal many things. His wife was more open; and I could read in her tightened lips and cold grey eyes, that she at least stood fast to the old quarrel. Cullingworth was little changed, and seemed to be as sanguine and as full of spirits as ever.

"Sound as a trout, my boy!" he cried, drumming on his chest with his hands. "Played for the London Scottish in their opening match last week, and was on the ball from whistle to whistle. Not so quick on a sprint - you find that yourself, Munro, eh what? - but a good hard-working bullocky forward. Last match I shall have for many a day, for I am off to South America next week."

"You have given up Bradfield altogether then?"

"Too provincial, my boy! What's the good of a village practice with a miserable three thousand or so a year for a man that wants room to spread? My head was sticking out at one end of Bradfield and my feet at the other. Why, there wasn't room for Hetty in the place, let alone me! I've taken to the eye, my boy. There's a fortune in the eye. A man grudges a half-crown to cure his chest or his throat, but he'd spend his last dollar over his eye. There's money in ears, but the eye is a gold mine."

"What!" said I, "in South America?"

"Just exactly in South America," he cried, pacing with his quick little steps up and down the dingy room. "Look here, laddie! There's a great continent from the equator to the icebergs, and not a man in it who could correct an astigmatism. What do they know of modern eye-surgery and refraction? Why, dammy, they don't know much about it in the provinces of England yet, let alone Brazil. Man, if you could only see it, there's a fringe of squinting millionaires sitting ten deep round the whole continent with their money in their hands waiting for an oculist. Eh, Munro, what? By Crums, I'll come back and I'll buy Bradfield, and I'll give it away as a tip to a waiter."

"You propose to settle in some large city, then?"

"City! What use would a city be to me? I'm there to squeeze the continent. I work a town at a time. I send on an agent to the next to say that I am coming. I `Here's the chance of a lifetime,' says he, `no need to go back to Europe. Here's Europe come to you. Squints, cataracts, iritis, refractions, what you like; here's the great Signor Cullingworth, right up to date and ready for anything!' In they come of course, droves of them, and then I arrive and take the money. Here's my luggage!" he pointed to two great hampers in the corner of the room. "Those are glasses, my boy, concave and convex, hundreds of them. I test an eye, fit him on the spot, and send him away shouting. Then I load up a steamer and come home, unless I elect to buy one of their little States and run it."

Of course it sounded absurd as he put it; but I could soon see that he had worked out his details, and that there was a very practical side to his visions.

"I work Bahia," said he. "My agent prepares Pernambuco. When Bahia is squeezed dry I move on to Pernambuco, and the agent ships to Monte Video. So we work our way round with a trail of spectacles behind us. "It'll go like clock-work."

"You will need to speak Spanish," said I.

"Tut, it does not take any Spanish to stick a knife into a man's eye. All I shall want to know is, `Money down - no credit.' That's Spanish enough for me."

We had a long and interesting talk about all that had happened to both of us, without, however, any allusion to our past quarrel. He would not admit that he had left Bradfield on account of a falling-off in his practice, or for any reason except that he found the place too small. His spring-screen invention had, he said, been favourably reported upon by one of the first private ship-building firms on the Clyde, and there was every probability of their adopting it.

"As to the magnet," said he, " I'm very sorry for my country, but there is no more command of the seas for her. I'll have to let the thing go to the Germans. It's not my fault. They must not blame me when the smash comes. I put the thing before the Admiralty, and I could have made a board school understand it in half the time. Such letters, Munro! Colney Hatch on blue paper. When the war comes, and I show those letters, somebody will be hanged. Questions about this - questions about that. At last they asked me what I proposed to fasten my magnet to. I answered to any solid impenetrable object, such as the head of an Admiralty official. Well, that broke the whole thing up. They wrote with their compliments, and they were returning my apparatus. I wrote with my compliments, and they might go to the devil. And so ends a great historical incident, Munro - eh, what? "

We parted very good friends, but with reservations, I fancy, on both sides. His last advice to me was to clear out of Birchespool.

"You can do better - you can do better, laddie!" said he. "Look round the whole world, and when you see a little round hole, jump in feet foremost. There's a lot of 'em about if a man keeps himself ready."

So those were the last words of Cullingworth, and the last that I may ever see of him also, for he starts almost immediately upon his strange venture. He must succeed. He is a man whom nothing could hold down. I wish him luck, and have a kindly feeling towards him, and yet I distrust him from the bottom of my heart, and shall be just as pleased to know that the Atlantic rolls between us.

Well, my dear Bertie, a happy and tranquil, if not very ambitious existence stretches before us. We are both in our twenty-fifth year, and I suppose that without presumption we can reckon that thirty-five more years lie in front of us. I can foresee the gradually increasing routine of work, the wider circle of friends, the indentification with this or that local movement, with perhaps a seat on the Bench, or at least in the Municipal Council in my later years. It's not a very startling programme, is it? But it lies to my hand, and I see no other. I should dearly love that the world should be ever so little better for my presence. Even on this small stage we have our two sides, and something might be done by throwing all one's weight on the scale of breadth, tolerance, charity, temperance, peace, and kindliness to man and beast. We can't all strike very big blows, and even the little ones count for something.

So good-bye, my dear boy, and remember that when you come to England our home would be the brighter for your presence. In any case, now that I have your address, I shall write again in a very few weeks. My kindest regards to Mrs. Swanborough.

Yours ever,

J. STARK MUNRO.

[This is the last letter which I was destined to receive from my poor friend. He started to spend the Christmas of that year (1884) with his people, and on the journey was involved in the fatal railroad accident at Sittingfleet, where the express ran into a freight train which was standing in the depot. Dr. and Mrs. Munro were the only occupants of the car next the locomotive, and were killed instantly, as were the brakesman and one other passenger. It was such an end as both he and his wife would have chosen; and no one who knew them would regret that neither was left to mourn the other. His insurance policy of eleven hundred pounds was sufficient to provide for the wants of his own family, which, as his father was sick, was the one worldly matter which could have caused him concern. - H. S.

Breinigsville, PA USA
11 January 2011
253044BV00001B/275/A